Antique

Antique SPEAK

**A Guide to the Styles, Techniques,
and Materials of the Decorative Arts,
from the Renaissance to Art Deco**

**Kathryn B. HIESINGER
and George H. MARCUS**

Abbeville Press   Publishers   New York   London   Paris

CONTENTS

Style	Timeline (1300–1900)	Dates
HISPANO-MORESQUE		1300s–1500s
RENAISSANCE		1400–1600
TUDOR		1485–1603
FRANCIS I		1515–1547
BAROQUE		1600–1700
JACOBEAN		1603–1649
LOUIS XIV		1643–1715
RESTORATION		1660–1688
WILLIAM AND MARY		1689–1702
QUEEN ANNE		1702–1714
GEORGIAN		1714–1811
RÉGENCE		1715–1723
LOUIS XV		1715–1774
ROCOCO		1720s–1770s
CHIPPENDALE		1750s–1780s
NEOCLASSICISM		1750s–1840s
GOTHIC REVIVAL		1750s–1870s
ADAM		1760s–1790s
LOUIS XVI		1774–1793
HEPPLEWHITE		1780s–1800s
FEDERAL		1789–1830s
SHERATON		1790s–1800s
EMPIRE		1804–1815
REGENCY		1811–1820
BIEDERMEIER		1815–1830s
CHARLES X		1824–1830
LOUIS-PHILIPPE		1830–1848
ROCOCO REVIVAL		1830s–1870s
RENAISSANCE REVIVAL		1830s–1880s
VICTORIAN		1837–1901
SECOND EMPIRE		1852–1870
ARTS AND CRAFTS MOVEMENT		1860s–1910s
AESTHETIC MOVEMENT		1870s–1880s
COLONIAL REVIVAL		1870s–1920s
ART NOUVEAU		1890s–1910
SECESSION		1897–1910s
ART DECO		1910s–1930s
MODERNISM		1920s–1930s

Understanding antiques requires knowledge of a specialized vocabulary that tells initiates what something is, where it came from, and when it was made. Lacking this language impedes serious discussion. Yet how many people know what is Empire about a sofa or the difference between a knotted or a woven carpet? Or what is Louis XIV or Louis-Philippe, porcelain, or pottery? Even experts in one area can be tripped up by the intricacies of another, and the definition of *antique* itself is imprecise. That is why this book can be very helpful to amateurs and professionals alike.

The essays in *AntiqueSpeak* discuss European and American styles (such as BAROQUE and ART DECO), materials (GLASS, IVORY), types of objects (FURNITURE, TOYS AND GAMES), specialized areas of collecting (EXPORT WARES, JUDAICA), and processes related to acquiring and caring for antiques (AUCTIONS, CONDITION). Each term is explained in a concise survey of the subject, and the essays are arranged in alphabetical order.

The essays that define styles—the set of constant characteristics that give sufficient coherence to an artistic expression of a group or period to make it recognizable and distinguishable from others—are divided into the journalistic categories of *Who, When, Where,* and *What.*

WHO is a list of the principal architects, artists, designers, craftsmen, manufacturers, and theorists. Certain individuals and companies appear in several entries, sometimes working in different countries, during different periods, and in different styles.

WHEN signifies the moment of greatest vitality for a particular style. The entry for ROCOCO REVIVAL, for example, gives the dates 1830s through 1870s, but the style continued in certain circles long after that. When the style has the name of a monarch, however, the reign dates for the monarch have been cited to avoid confusion, even though in many cases the characteristics of the style were apparent before the reign began and persisted strongly after it was over.

WHERE identifies the countries or continents in which a style was centered. It does not mean that artists and craftsmen involved in that style did not live or work in other places, nor that the style did not eventually travel to other areas.

WHAT defines the origins, nature, and implications of the style. As can be seen from these entries, the history of European styles (at least those following the Renaissance) was centered in France and England, and many styles take their names from the monarchs of these countries. This is not a case of Franco- or Anglophilia. From the mid-seventeenth to the early twentieth century in Europe, France set the styles and the rest of the Continent followed, so that it is not at all uncommon to see references to "Spanish Louis XV" or "Russian Empire" objects. Even though many influences came to England from France, British decorative arts had a separate line of development with its own versions and sequence of styles, which were also diffused throughout its colonies. Thus in colonial America the styles followed the same forms and nomenclature as those used in England.

What is the best way to use this volume? That depends on who you are. *AntiqueSpeak* has been designed for different kinds of users and different situations. Confronted with a particular antique object, a reader might want to look up its period, decoration, and material (for example, ROCOCO, CHINOISERIE, GOLD AND SILVER). The student, collector, and inveterate antique hunter will find it useful to read the book from beginning to end, then return to it as needed, guidebook fashion. A StyleChart puts the material in chronological perspective; cross-references and an extensive index (which provides dates for the figures discussed in the book) ensure easy access to additional information. The purpose of all these elements is to offer the reader an unintimidating way to become familiar with the language of antiques.

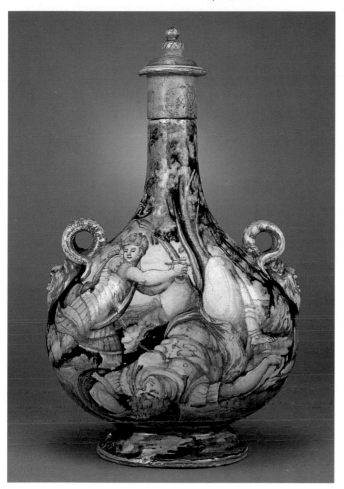

Flask or Flagon, c. 1545–50. Made in Urbino, Italy. Majolica, height: 13³/₄ in. (35 cm). The Wallace Collection, London.

Embroidered Box, 1662. English. Silk and metallic threads on satin, seed pearls, wood, and metal, 11¾ x 11 x 8 in. (29.8 x 27.9 x 20.3 cm). The Minneapolis Institute of Arts; The John Van R. Van Derlip Fund and gifts in honor of Mary Ann Butterfield.

Carpet, 1670–77. Woven at the royal Savonnerie manufactory, Paris. Wool and linen, 26 ft. 3 in. x 18 ft. 6 in. (4.95 x 5.64 m). Philadelphia Museum of Art; Bequest of Eleanore Elkins Rice.

ANDRÉ-CHARLES BOULLE (1642–1732).
Cabinet, c. 1700. French. Pine, oak, walnut, and ebony with marquetry of brass, pewter, tortoiseshell, and colored woods, gilt-bronze mounts, and marble, height: 73 1/2 in. (187 cm). Musée du Louvre, Paris; On deposit from the Mobilier National.

ROBERT ADAM (1728–1792).
Armchair, 1765. Made by Thomas Chippendale, London. Gilded wood,
height: 36 in. (91.4 cm). Aske Hall, Yorkshire, England.

JUSTE-AURÈLE MEISSONNIER (1695–1750).
Candelabrum, 1734–35. Made by Claude Duvivier, Paris. Silver, height: 15¼ in.
(39 cm). Musée des Arts Décoratifs, Paris.

Broth Basin, Cover, and Stand, c. 1800. Made by the Real Fabbrica
Ferdinandea, Naples. Soft-paste porcelain with enamel and gilt decoration,
diameter of stand: 9 in. (22.5 cm). Victoria and Albert Museum, London

MARTIN CARLIN (c. 1730–1785).
Writing Table, c. 1776. French. Oak veneered with rosewood and amaranth,
gilt-bronze mounts, and soft-paste Sèvres porcelain plaques, height: 46 in.
(117 cm). The Wallace Collection, London.

Attributed to **WILLIAM SINCLAIR** (1775–1826).
Writing Desk, c. 1801–5. American. Mahogany and satinwood with ivory escutcheons, wood inlay, and mirrors, 59 1/2 x 30 1/2 x 19 3/4 in. (151.1 x 77.5 x 50.2 cm). Philadelphia Museum of Art; Bequest of Miss Fanny Norris in memory of Louis Marie Clapier.

MARTIN-GUILLAUME BIENNAIS (1764–1843).
Perfume Burner or Jardiniere (Athénienne), 1800–1804. French. Yew, bronze, and silver, height: 35¹/₂ in. (90 cm). Musée du Louvre, Paris.

CHARLES MEIGH (active 1835–51).
Apostle Teapot and Jug, 1842. Made by Old Hall Pottery, Hanley,
Staffordshire, England. Salt-glaze stoneware, jug height: 10⅝ in. (27.2 cm),
teapot height: 6⅞ in. (17.5 cm). Philadelphia Museum of Art;
Gift of Mrs. Alfred Percival Smith.

Attributed to **JOHN HENRY BELTER** (1804–1863).
Side Chair, 1855. American. Rosewood, height: 44¼ in. (112.4 cm). The Metropolitan Museum of Art, New York; Gift of Mr. and Mrs. Lowell Ross Burch and Jean McLean Morron.

EDOUARD MÜLLER (1823–1876).
The Garden of Armida, c. 1855. Printed by Jules Desfossé, Paris.
Block-printed wallpaper, 12 ft. 8 in. x 11 ft. (3.86 x 3.35 m). Philadelphia
Museum of Art; Gift (by exchange) of Julia G. Fahnestock in memory of
her husband, William Fahnestock.

WILLIAM MORRIS (1834–1896).
Bullerswood Carpet, 1889. English. Wool, 24¹/2 ft. x 12 ft. 9¹/4 in.
(7.47 x 3.89 m). Victoria and Albert Museum, London.

HECTOR GUIMARD (1867–1942).
Jardiniere, 1902–3. Made by the Manufacture Nationale de Sèvres. Glazed stoneware, height: 51⁵⁄₈ in. (131 cm). Manufacture Nationale de Sèvres, Sèvres, France.

ALBERT CHEURET (n.d.).
Clock, c. 1930. French. Silvered bronze and onyx, 6½ x 16½ x 4 in.
(15.9 x 41.9 x 10.1 cm). Virginia Museum of Fine Arts, Richmond; Gift of Sydney
and Frances Lewis.

ORNAMENTS

ACANTHUS

ANTHEMION

ARABESQUE

CARTOUCHE

CROCKETS

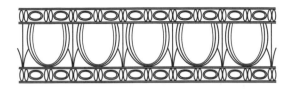

CARYATID

EGG AND DART

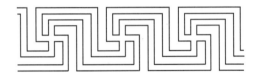

FESTOON

FRET

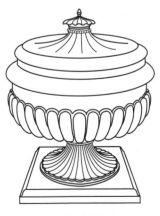

GADROON

GRIFFIN

HERM

HUSKS

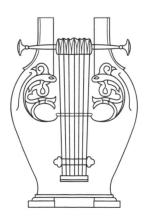

LYRE

PALMETTE

PATERAE

PINNACLE

C SCROLL

S SCROLL

STRAPWORK

TRACERY

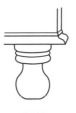

BALL

BRACKET

CLAW AND BALL

HOOFED

PAD, OR CLUB

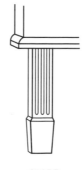

PAW

SCROLL

SPADE

DORIC   **IONIC**   **CORINTHIAN**

ADAM

▷ **WHO** Robert Adam

▷ **WHEN** 1760s through 1790s

▷ **WHERE** Great Britain and America

▷ **WHAT** The Adam style of architecture, interior design, and furnishing is identified with the Scottish architect Robert Adam, who, assisted by his brother James, adapted and mixed elements from antiquity in an original synthesis that became one of the strands of NEOCLASSICISM. Light and elegant in mood and refined in execution, the Adam interior was conceived as a unified decorative scheme. Spaces were geometric, with niches and semicircular recesses, and the ancient classical orders of columns and pilasters were used to outline them. Walls and ceilings were typically decorated, in paint and relief, with an intricate profusion of small motifs. These included tripod candelabra, arabesques, tendrils, roundels, sphinxes, nereids, and tritons, which were organized in slender vertical pilasters, geometric panels, and allover surface patterns.

The same ornamental vocabulary was applied to the mirrors, chimneypieces, overmantels, furniture, and carpets that Adam designed for his interiors, which were made to his designs by the London cabinetmakers Ince and Mayhew and John Linnell and by the carpet firm of Thomas Moore, among others. Similar forms and motifs also appeared during the 1770s and 1780s in the metalwork of Matthew Boulton and the ceramics of Josiah Wedgwood. The Adam style was spread to the United States during the FEDERAL period through Robert and James Adam's *Works in Architecture,* a three-volume compendium illustrating designs for furniture and interiors as well as buildings, published between 1773 and 1822. The 1870s and 1880s saw a revival of the Adam style in England, where cabinetmaking firms such as Holland and Sons produced furniture with painted Adamesque decorations.

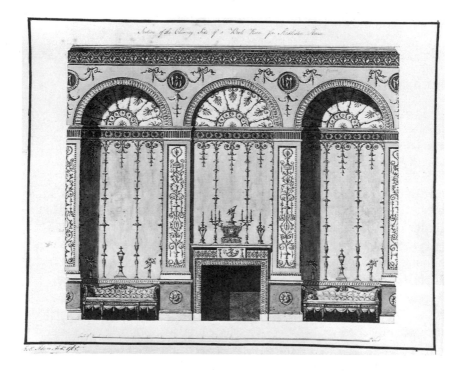

ROBERT ADAM (1728–1792).
Design for a Book Room for Kedleston, 1768. English. Pen, ink, and wash on paper, 14¹/2 x 20¹/4 in. (36.2 x 51.4 cm). Kedleston Hall, Derbyshire, England; National Trust Photographic Library.

AESTHETIC MOVEMENT

▷ **WHO** ARCHITECTS, ARTISTS, AND DESIGNERS: G. F. Bodley; Lewis F. Day; Christopher Dresser; Charles Locke Eastlake; E. W. Godwin; John La Farge; McKim, Mead, and White; Richard Norman Shaw; Bruce J. Talbert; Philip Webb; James McNeill Whistler
CRAFTSMEN AND MANUFACTURERS: Herter Brothers, Liberty & Co., Louis Comfort Tiffany

▷ **WHEN** 1870s to 1880s

▷ **WHERE** Great Britain and the United States

▷ **WHAT** The Aesthetic movement sought to reform architecture and the decorative arts by promoting theories of "art for art's sake" and lighter, simpler, more graceful designs. These included the revival of QUEEN ANNE redbrick buildings with chaste exterior decoration and picturesque silhouettes of gables and tall chimneys; "art" furniture (often black or ebonized) that was simple, rectilinear, and lightweight, with slender, turned uprights, and shallow-carved ornament; and interiors in subdued, closely related colors, typically decorated with wallpapers in delicate floral patterns. The Aesthetic movement was rooted in the antipathy many designers and critics felt in the mid-nineteenth century for the poor quality of British industrial products; it was embodied in the reforms they conceived, including those of John Ruskin and of William Morris, whose ARTS AND CRAFTS MOVEMENT overlapped the Aesthetic movement in certain respects. The social and educational aspects of the Aesthetic movement were particularly evident in the increasing numbers of books designed especially for children, such as those by Walter Crane, Kate Greenaway, and others.

The simply designed and beautifully crafted Japanese objects shown in London at the International Exhibition of 1862 provided the Aesthetic movement with its most inspiring example of what art should be, as did the increasing imports of Japanese woodblock prints, lacquerwares, pottery, and other products. Japanese forms and subjects were widely adopted by British manufacturers and designers in all mediums, and the resulting craze ranged from Wedgwood pottery decorated with fans, sparrows, and plum blossoms to electroplated teapots by Christopher Dresser in straight-sided and angular shapes.

Among the most notorious (and satirized) Aesthetic movement admirers of things Japanese were the British writer Oscar Wilde and the American

E. W. GODWIN (1833–1886).
Sideboard, c. 1867. English. Made by William Watt. Ebonized wood, with silver-plated fittings and Japanese leather paper, 71 x 102 x 22 in. (180 x 259 x 55.9 cm). Victoria and Albert Museum, London.

painter James McNeill Whistler. Whistler's Peacock Room of 1876–77 (now in the Freer Gallery, Smithsonian Institution, Washington, D.C.)—a dining room decorated with gold peacocks on a blue ground in imitation of Japanese *makie* lacquers for his patron Frederick Richards Leyland—is considered an apogee of the style, as was Whistler's own house in London, decorated and furnished in the 1880s by E. W. Godwin. The British achievements in Aesthetic movement design were rapidly absorbed in the United States through contemporary publications on furniture and decoration, among them Charles Locke Eastlake's *Hints on Household Taste* (1868) and Bruce J. Talbert's *Gothic Forms* (1867), and furthered by Wilde's lecture tour in 1882–83. American books and magazines advised their readers how to make their homes more artistic while firms such as Herter Brothers and Louis Comfort Tiffany supplied Aesthetic interiors with objects notable for their craftsmanship and surface ornamentation.

ANTIQUES

Antiques belong to what are generally called the "decorative," or "applied," arts (as opposed to fine arts such as painting and sculpture), and the term *antiques* simply refers to old objects within this category. The United States Customs Service provides a stricter—and the only legal American—definition of an antique, but this has jurisdiction only over articles being brought into this country. The *Code of Federal Regulations* (19 CFR 10.53) defines *antiques* as "movable articles of convenience or decoration for use in furnishing a house, apartment, place of business or accommodation," with the essential requirement for free entry as an antique being that "the article is not less than 100 years of age."

Despite this age restriction, the term is used much more broadly and loosely by dealers, collectors, and the press, and has been for the past several centuries. Sidestepping the issue of age, the National Antique and Art Dealers Association of America includes dealers in twentieth-century decorative arts among its members. A number of antique shows also encompass more recent objects, under the label *modernism,* which are defined by style rather than age, such as works from the ARTS AND CRAFTS MOVEMENT through the 1960s. *Design* (from *industrial design*) is another term applied to objects from the nineteenth and twentieth centuries, usually those generated for machine production that follow modernist principles, but it has also been extended to cover handmade ornamental and craft objects made since the beginning of this century.

Collectibles, another category of decorative and useful objects as well as ephemera, most often refers to cheaply made, mass-produced, and mass-marketed articles from the present, as well as older articles that may have been neglected by historians and collectors in the past (for example, trade cards and other types of early advertising). Collectibles are seldom prized for the aesthetic qualities that distinguish antiques. But, like stamps and some coins, they are nonetheless collected passionately, with some, such as sports memorabilia and commemorative plates, attaining significant prices.

APPLIQUÉ—*see* NEEDLEWORK

ART DECO

▷ **WHO** ARCHITECTS AND DESIGNERS: A. M. Cassandre, Pierre Chareau, Donald Deskey, Marion Dorn, Raoul Dufy, Jean-Michel Frank, Paul T. Frankl, Eileen Gray, Paul Poiret, Pierre Selmersheim, Joseph Urban, William Van Alen, Kem Weber
CRAFTSMEN AND MANUFACTURERS: Rose Adler, Edouard Bénédictus, Edgar Brandt, Albert Cheuret, Marcel Coard, Ivan da Silva Bruhns, François-Emile Décorchement, Maurice Dufrène, Jean Dunand, Paul Follot, Jean Goulden, André Groult, Paul Iribe, René Lalique, Pierre Legrain, Claudius Linossier, Maurice Marinot, Clément Mère, Jean Perzel, Eugène Printz, Jean Puiforcat, Armand-Albert Rateau, Clément Rousseau, Emile-Jacques Ruhlmann, Eugene Schoen, Süe et Mare (Louis Süe and André Mare), Raymond Templier

▷ **WHEN** 1910s to 1930s

▷ **WHERE** Europe (particularly France) and the United States

▷ **WHAT** The last in the sequence of broadly influential international styles that arose in France, Art Deco spoke in a Cubism-inspired, Jazz Age idiom that was also deeply informed by the elegant shapes and fine craftsmanship of the eighteenth century, particularly the LOUIS XV and LOUIS XVI periods. This bold and colorful geometric style first appeared before World War I and was fully elaborated afterward, reaching its high point in 1925 in the pavilions and furnishings designed for the *Exposition internationale des arts décoratifs et industriels modernes* in Paris (the source of the term *Art Deco*). Unlike the unornamented, mechanistic style of MODERNISM, which was being created contemporaneously by architects, the opulent Art Deco style was the work of designer-decorators *(ensembliers).* Their overarching vision of a plush, elegant modernity bestowed a stylistic unity on the decorative arts of their time. Using a team of designers, artists, and artisans, the firms of such decorators and craftsmen as Emile-Jacques Ruhlmann, Süe et Mare, and Paul Poiret (working independently) and Paul Follot and Maurice Dufrène (working for the decorating studios of department stores) provided clients with an ensemble of carpets, furniture, fabrics, lighting, paintings and sculpture, and decorative accessories for the furnishing of domestic and commercial interiors. These decorators were also able to broadcast their style publicly, for they received state commissions to fit out government buildings, embassies, railroad interiors, and the great ocean liners that were the pride of France.

Art Deco design was not directly imitative of historical styles, but it did bring the values of the eighteenth and early nineteenth centuries into a modern mode, with its vocabulary of swags, tassels, flowers, vases, and fruits; traditional FURNITURE techniques of veneering and marquetry; and lavish use of costly materials, such as exotic woods, ivory and mother-of-pearl inlays, gilt-bronze mounts, LACQUER finishes, and sharkskin (shagreen) upholstery. The craftsmanship of past centuries was also recalled in the ornamental ironwork by Edgar Brandt and Armand-Albert Rateau, *pâte de verre* vessels by François-Emile Décorchement, silver by Jean Puiforcat, patinated metalwork by Claudius Linossier, and enamels by Jean Goulden.

The impact of Art Deco was quickly felt abroad, throughout Europe and from Turkey to Thailand, as wealthy clients commissioned French designers to transport the latest in Parisian decoration to their own lands. When Art Deco came to the United States, where it was first championed by department stores and émigré designers such as Paul T. Frankl and Kern Weber, it merged with elements of European modernism and American skyscraper design to form an independent variant known then as Art Moderne. Best exemplified by William Van Alen's Chrysler Building and Donald Deskey's interior for Radio City Music Hall in New York, this style had a monumental scale and decorative exuberance. From architecture and interiors it spread to industrial design in the guise of gleaming appliances, plastic radios, and glass and metal furnishings, as well as to the products of Grand Rapids, Michigan, which offered the American public veneered furniture with streamlined shapes, round mirrors, and the latest in metal and plastic hardware.

ART MODERNE—*see* ART DECO

ART NOUVEAU

▷ **WHO** ARCHITECTS AND DESIGNERS: August Endell, Antoni Gaudí, Hector Guimard, Josef Hoffmann, Victor Horta, Charles Rennie Mackintosh, Koloman Moser, Hermann Obrist, Richard Riemerschmid, Henry van de Velde, Otto Wagner
CRAFTSMEN AND MANUFACTURERS: Emile Gallé, René Lalique, Liberty & Co., Louis Majorelle, Louis Comfort Tiffany

▷ **WHEN** 1890s to 1910

▷ **WHERE** Europe and the United States

▷ **WHAT** Art Nouveau—a self-consciously "new" style of sinuous, curving lines often associated with plant forms—took its name from the art gallery that Siegfried Bing opened in Paris in 1895. The style was called Jugendstil in Germany, Secessionstil (see SECESSION) in Austria, and Stile Liberty in Italy. It was applied universally to architecture and design, including domestic furnishings, textiles, jewelry, and posters. Art Nouveau intended to express its own time, both in an original formal language without historical precedents and in the use of modern materials and machine techniques. Victor Horta in Belgium and Hector Guimard in France used uncamouflaged cast iron in their architecture, without reference to past styles; the Vereinigte Werkstätten für Kunst im Handwerk (United Workshops for Art in Handicrafts) in Munich and the Wiener Werkstätte (Vienna Workshop) relied both on craft techniques and on machine production, as did independent artist-makers like Emile Gallé in France and Louis Comfort Tiffany in the United States, who mass-produced commercial lines of glass alongside their handmade luxury products. Art Nouveau architects used the new style to unify all parts of their buildings in structure and decoration. In his Castel Béranger apartment building in Paris (1894–98), Guimard repeated whiplash lines over walls, floors, ceilings, windows, lighting fixtures, wallpaper, and furniture.

Like artists connected with the ARTS AND CRAFTS MOVEMENT, the Art Nouveau designers placed importance on useful, everyday objects, both as a means of self-expression and as essential to the creation of a visually unified environment. Some, like Henry van de Velde, were inspired by the example of William Morris to build and furnish their own houses; others, like Richard Riemerschmid and Hermann Obrist, who founded the workshops in Munich (1897), and Josef Hoffmann and Koloman Moser, who founded the workshop in Vienna (1903), established commercial enterprises. Again inspired by Morris—whose company sold furniture, textiles, wallpapers, and other goods—and by the products of other Arts and Crafts groups and collaborative workshops, Art Nouveau designers tried to create well-designed and well-made "artistic" products that would satisfy and uplift craftsman and consumer alike.

The work of the glassmakers Gallé in France and Tiffany in the United States (who also designed furniture and metalwork, respectively) embodied the most naturalistic side of Art Nouveau; both described flowering plants and insects in their richly complex glass; other artists, such as Obrist and van de Velde, worked in a more abstract vocabulary that anticipated aspects of MODERNISM. Still others stood stylistically between Art Nouveau and Arts and Crafts—notably Charles Rennie Mackintosh, who in the interiors he designed and furnished in Glasgow combined rectilinear forms and simple wood constructions with stylized floral motifs and curves.

Easily imitated in cheaply manufactured products, Art Nouveau ran its course by World War I, when its deliberate artfulness and ornamentalism lost favor to simpler, less decorative styles. It was the first modern style to be revived in this century (by Italian architects and designers in the late 1950s), and its best products became widely collected after museums in Zurich (Kunstgewerbemuseum, 1952) and New York (Museum of Modern Art, 1959) popularized the style in major exhibitions.

ARTS AND CRAFTS MOVEMENT

▷ **WHO** ARCHITECTS, ARTISTS, AND DESIGNERS: C. R. Ashbee, Ford Madox Brown, Edward Burne-Jones, Walter Crane, Charles Sumner Greene, Henry Mather Greene, John La Farge, W. R. Lethaby, A. H. Mackmurdo, William Morris, Dante Gabriel Rossetti, C. F. A. Voysey, Philip Webb
CRAFTSMEN AND MANUFACTURERS: W. A. S. Benson, William De Morgan, William H. Grueby, Elbert Hubbard, Harry J. Powell, Rookwood Pottery, Gustav Stickley
THEORIST: John Ruskin

▷ **WHEN** 1860s through 1910s

▷ **WHERE** Great Britain and the United States

▷ **WHAT** The Arts and Crafts movement was founded on the socialist theories of John Ruskin and William Morris, who advocated improving the design and manufacture of domestic products through artistic handicraft, thereby bettering the lives of craftsmen and their clients—in Morris's words, an "art of the people, by the people, and for the people." Like the AESTHETIC MOVEMENT, it sought the integration of art into life, placing high value on beauty in everyday objects. Morris himself put theory to practice in the workshop and retail firm he established in 1861 (Morris, Marshall, Faulkner and Co.; later, Morris and Co.), which made and sold furniture, tiles, metalwork, jewelry, embroideries, and stained glass after his own designs and those by his partners: Edward Burne-Jones, Ford Madox Brown, Dante Gabriel Rossetti, and Philip Webb. The resulting objects were largely produced by traditional craft techniques that were intended to show an "honest" and purposeful use of materials. Some of the firm's products were made by outside suppliers, including Jeffrey and Company for wallpapers, and Clarksons and Thomas Wardle for printed textiles. In 1881 Morris set up his own looms and print works for textiles at Merton Abbey in Surrey, where he also wove TAPESTRIES and CARPETS.

Taking a stance with Ruskin against modern industry and machine production (although he designed machine-made carpets for several commercial firms), Morris found inspiration in historical styles and was also a force in the GOTHIC REVIVAL. The designs of his firm were often based on medieval prototypes as well as on RENAISSANCE, BAROQUE, and later examples. Morris was known particularly for his hand-blocked WALLPAPER and textiles, with designs that include birds, animals, and flowers set among intertwined stems and foliage; the principal motifs are often repeated in mirrored pairs or back to back and arranged in alternating horizontal bands, as in a medieval *verdure* tapestry. Probably the firm's most commercially successful product was its "Sussex" furniture—light, portable, and utilitarian, with simple turned parts, ebonized finishes, and rush seats. It was developed from a COUNTRY prototype found in Sussex (the descendant of a so-called fancy SHERATON chair), which, with its rush seat and spindles, depended in turn on medieval traditions of chair making. The reclining armchair with a fixed seat and a hinged back—known in America as the "Morris chair"—was similarly developed by the firm from a vernacular prototype from Sussex.

Inspired by Morris's ideas and example, several organizations were founded in London to promote the craft aesthetic. Most important was the Arts and Crafts Exhibition Society, which gave its name to the movement. Its members included Walter Crane, W. A. S. Benson, Morris, Webb, and William De Morgan, and its exhibitions were held in London from 1888 to 1916. The Century Guild, founded by A. H. Mackmurdo in 1882, produced work designed and executed by guild members, which was published in the guild's journal, the *Hobby Horse*. The Art Workers' Guild, a discussion group, was formed in 1884 for the interchange of ideas among architects and designers.

The Guild and School of Handicraft, founded by C. R. Ashbee in 1888, produced furniture, jewelry, and silverware. Their silver was made for both private and ecclesiastic clients, each piece individual, often hand hammered, and decorated with stylized naturalistic motifs characteristic of ART NOUVEAU. Ashbee's work became well known abroad: it was published in the *Studio* and shown in exhibitions of the Arts and Crafts Exhibition Society and in Germany, France, and Austria (see SECESSION).

Ashbee and Crane visited America several times, spreading Arts and Crafts ideals in various cities, including Chicago, where the Chicago Arts and Crafts Society was founded in 1897. American craftsmen and manufacturers also visited Great Britain; among them was Gustav Stickley, whose Craftsman Workshops was founded in Eastwood (near Syracuse), New York, in 1901, along Arts and Crafts lines and whose metalwork, textiles, and furniture were promoted in his *Craftsman* magazine. Simple in construction and materials, Stickley's early work (known by his contemporaries as "Mission" furniture because of its severity) was made of plain, undecorated oak boards. Like their British equivalents and contemporary Art Nouveau firms, American Arts and Crafts groups largely did not survive World War I.

AUCTIONS

Auctions are sales at which the prices of goods are determined by competitive bidding among a group of potential buyers. The highly organized form of auction familiar today in the field of art and antiques had its origins in eighteenth-century England, when many of the largest and best-known auction houses were founded, including Sotheby's (1744), Christie's (1766), and Phillips (1796). It was a form of public sale that both originated in and further encouraged the aristocratic cult of collecting in that country. One of the most spectacular series of auctions during that era, however, was held in France, where the possessions of the French royal family were put up for sale several years after the revolution of 1789.

Modern auctions take many forms, ranging from those that become major social and economic events, with great art and antique treasures catalogued in expensive illustrated volumes by major international auction houses, to those held outdoors or in tents in country settings, where the entire contents of a house, from furniture to garden tools, are put on the block (usually to settle an estate). While the methods and terms of auctions can vary from one firm to another, certain features are common for most. Before bidding, buyers are generally obliged to register and obtain a bidder's number so that they can be identified when their bid is accepted and a sale is completed. Many auction houses charge the buyer (as well as the seller) a premium above the selling or "hammer" price. A "lot" (each item or group of items sold as one) may be subject to a "reserve," a minimum price below which it will not be sold but instead will be "bought back" or "bought in." Other sales are unrestricted, with every lot sold regardless of the amount bid.

Although reputable auction houses take care to describe sale items correctly in terms of authorship and attribution, date, and CONDITION, they generally disclaim in writing any final responsibility for such descriptions. Therefore, buyers should always be fully acquainted with the terms of a sale before bidding and should carefully inspect the works they are considering, using their own judgment and that of trusted advisers, before entering into competition for items, which may be sold "as is." The competitive nature of auctions, which may result in a battle of opposing wills, means that human factors can play as much a role in determining price as the inherent value of the goods being sold. Buyers are generally advised to decide in advance exactly what they can pay for each lot, setting a price above which they will not go, so that in the heat of bidding they do not purchase items that cost more than the bidder can afford or more than they are worth. For catalog sales, low and high estimates of what an object might bring are printed in advance; at other sales, estimates may be given by agents of the auction house.

Bidders should be aware of possible auction abuses, such as "bidding to the room" (when auctioneers accept bids from phantom buyers to raise the price) or "pooling" (when a group of buyers agree to buy cheaply by not competing with each other, then settling among themselves afterward). A common misconception about auction records concerns the selective use of sale prices to establish the value of similar items without specifying the particular reasons (whether related to the individual buyer or the work's individual qualities) that accounted for the price. Any single auction price can never be as useful as the record of repeated sales over a period of time to determine the current value of an antique.

BAROQUE

▷ **WHO** ARCHITECTS, ARTISTS, AND DESIGNERS: Jean Berain, Gian Lorenzo Bernini, Francesco Borromini, Caravaggio, Annibale Carracci, Pietro da Cortona, Antoine Coysevox, François Duquesnoy, Carlo Fontana, François Girardon, Jules Hardouin-Mansart, Nicholas Hawksmoor, Charles Le Brun, Jean Lepautre, Louis Le Vau, Daniel Marot, Nicolas Poussin, Peter Paul

Rubens, Massimiliano Soldani, John Vanbrugh, Sir Anthony Van Dyck, Christopher Wren, Diego Velázquez

CRAFTSMEN AND MANUFACTURERS: André-Charles Boulle, Hans Coenraadt Breghtel, Andrea Brustolon, Grinling Gibbons, Adam van Vianen

▷ **WHEN** 1600 to 1700

▷ **WHERE** Europe and Latin America

▷ **WHAT** The Baroque style first appeared in Italy toward the end of the sixteenth century and spread throughout western Europe and Latin America during the seventeenth and early eighteenth centuries. The term probably derives from the Latin word for snail shell, suggesting the dynamism of the style, with its irregular, often complex curves and dramatic contrasts of light and dark. Different from the simple, orderly compositions of the RENAISSANCE, Baroque works express drama and emotion in exuberant, often grandiose effects that served the political ambitions of the rich and powerful churchmen and statesmen who commissioned them.

Architects, painters, and sculptors were the leading designers of courtly and ecclesiastical objects. They built, decorated, and luxuriously furnished churches and palaces (which could be immense)—including Gian Lorenzo Bernini's colonnaded square in front of Saint Peter's in Rome (begun 1656), the palace of Versailles by Louis Le Vau and Jules Hardouin-Mansart (1668–85), and the cathedral of Zacatecas in Mexico (dedicated 1752). In Spain, Diego Velázquez supervised renovations of the Alcázar palace for Philip IV (from 1647) and designed frescoes and tapestries for the state apartments. In France, Charles Le Brun directed the Manufacture Royale des Meubles de la Couronne (Royal Manufactory of Crown Furnishings) at the Gobelins factory for LOUIS XIV, where CARPETS, silver basins, inlaid tables, and other luxury articles were made. These included solid-silver furniture used at Versailles, which was imitated in Germany, Holland, and England (see GOLD AND SILVER).

Baroque luxury objects were made of the richest materials, often in combination, and display great refinement of workmanship. They include French FURNITURE by André-Charles Boulle (who gave his name to showy marquetry decorations of tortoiseshell and brass); Dutch tooled-and-gilded-leather wall coverings; Flemish cabinets of ebony, ivory, tortoiseshell, or oriental lacquerwork inlaid with mother-of-pearl; Italian cabinets of HARDSTONES, arranged in colorful pictorial mosaics; and German gold and silver work from

Augsburg in voluptuous forms with deeply embossed grotesque, floral, or acanthus decoration.

The Baroque style was spread by architects, painters, sculptors, and craftsmen who traveled or sent their work abroad. Bernini, for example, was called to France by Louis XIV to prepare designs for the Louvre palace (ultimately rejected), and the van Vianen family of Netherlandish silversmiths worked for the courts of Munich and Prague and for Charles I of England. In addition, ornamental engravings provided widely disseminated patterns for every conceivable kind of object. The spread of the Baroque style internationally was spurred by the revocation of the Edict of Nantes in 1685, which forced Huguenot craftsmen to leave France. Among them was Daniel Marot, who popularized French fashions abroad through his engraved designs for furniture and interior decoration and his work in Holland at the court of William of Orange and later in England, where William became king (see WILLIAM AND MARY).

BASKETRY

Few baskets survive that are more than two centuries old. Sturdy containers, they were made, and mended, with strong but impermanent natural materials such as straw, splint, cane, and willow. Baskets are difficult to document or date since basketry forms remained fairly constant over long periods and over large areas, with many European shapes and techniques having been transplanted intact to the New World. Native Americans, whose daily activities depended heavily on basketry, and European settlers in turn shared elements of their individual traditions, and aspects of their production are often difficult to distinguish. Even the highly prized SHAKER baskets, made in a great range of types for use in their communities and for sale to outsiders, follow mostly traditional forms, although they were executed with particular elegance and fine craftsmanship.

Baskets are made by coiling or by weaving. In coiling, tubular bundles of grasses or reeds bound with cord, bark, or similar materials are built up in a spiral to create circular forms, with each row stitched to the one below. Weaving is of two general types: wickerwork (weaving with willow rods or osiers, vines, twigs, or other plant fibers) and plaiting with splints (thin strips of wood split from hickory, oak, or ash logs). Simple woven patterns such as twills or herringbones are created by varying the number of warps crossed by each weft; color variations are also introduced by combining different materials, by using dyed splints, or by mixing rods with peeled and unpeeled bark.

Basket, 1800–1850. American, Shaker. Black ash, height: 12³/4 in. (32.4 cm). Philadelphia Museum of Art; Gift of Mr. and Mrs. Julius Zieget.

Baskets were commonly put to use in kitchen, garden, and laundry and served all the trades. Special forms evolved to fulfill particular functions, such as hexagonal-weave splint openwork cheese and curd baskets; flat winnowing sieves; large, rugged, footed, splint apple-gathering baskets; graduated, nesting measuring sets; and coiled conical beehives. VICTORIAN fancywork brought basketry into the parlor in the nineteenth century, with fine boxes and sewing baskets plaited of very thin, often imported, exotic fibers such as raffia and Chinese rice grass. Basketry techniques have also been used to make clothing, fans, cradles and baby carriages, and FURNITURE (notably the mass-produced wickerwork of the later nineteenth and early twentieth centuries).

BAUHAUS—*see* MODERNISM

BIEDERMEIER

▷ **WHO** ARCHITECTS AND DESIGNERS: Leo von Klenze, Karl Friedrich Schinkel CRAFTSMEN AND MANUFACTURERS: Dominik Biemann, Josef Ulrich Danhauser, Friedrich Egermann, Johann Conrad Geiss, Franz Gottstein, Anton Kothgasser, Gottlob Samuel Mohn

▷ **WHEN** 1815 through 1830s

▷ **WHERE** Germany, Austria, central Europe, and Scandinavia

▷ **WHAT** The first fashionable European style that was directed as much to the middle class as to an aristocratic clientele, Biedermeier flourished within the Germanic nations and Scandinavia from the defeat of Napoleon to the mid-1830s. As a late expression of NEOCLASSICISM, it incorporated elements of the LOUIS XVI, EMPIRE, CHARLES X, and late SHERATON styles. Its name—originally derogatory and applied only after the fact—was taken from that of a mid-nineteenth-century pseudonymous author of comic poems, Gottlieb Biedermeier, who represented all that was solid and stolid in the German bourgeois life of the period. Out of fashion during the second half of the nineteenth century, the Biedermeier style was rediscovered by art historians as well as designers, including those of the SECESSION at the turn of the twentieth century, but a wider interest in it has emerged only in the last decades.

Most characteristic of the style is its simple, light-colored, architectonic furniture with contrasting decoration applied amid broad expanses of veneer. Biedermeier furniture was practical, often multipurpose, and charm-

KNTIQ

BIEDERMEIER

DOMINIK BIEMANN (1800–1857).
Lidded Tumbler, 1830–31. Made in Bohemia. Cut and engraved crystal glass, with silver-gilt decoration, height: 6⅞ in. (17.5 cm). Kunstsammlung der Veste Coburg, Coburg, Germany.

ingly domestic in scale, with chests, secretary cabinets, and open, curved-back chairs being its most representative forms. Its decorative vocabulary included columns, pilasters, lyres, caryatids, herms, animal feet, and swans, as well as Egyptian Revival heads and sphinxes, which were, however, used sparingly. Few makers' names can be attached to this furniture, for it was usually designed by anonymous craftsmen, whose only signatures were their evident delight in the richness they could achieve with their materials, particularly wood grains, and the quality of their workmanship.

Biedermeier glass from the numerous factories in Bohemia was celebrated internationally and exported throughout the world. Cut in broad, flat panels and often deeply colored, these glasswares were decorated with engraving and enamel painting, done by specialists outside the factories. Tumblers, notably the smooth, thick-based *Ranftbecher,* were engraved with profile portraits or scenes from printed engravings by craftsmen such as Dominik Biemann of Prague or painted by artists such as Anton Kothgasser of Vienna with landscapes, monuments, flowers, or symbols and inscriptions of friend-ship and love. These were bought in great quantities for presentation and as travel remembrances. Porcelain cups and saucers—made by factories in Berlin, Dresden, Fürstenberg, Nymphenburg, and Vienna and painted with a similar range of subjects—also enjoyed a lively commerce as souvenirs and gifts.

BRASS

Yellowish in color, brass is an alloy of COPPER and zinc that is stronger and tougher than pure copper and also malleable (easy to shape), ductile (able to be drawn into thin wires without breaking), and fusible (easily melted). Until about the eighteenth century, the term *brass* was used interchangeably with BRONZE to describe copper alloys, which were also known simply as copper. Almost any method used for shaping metal can be used to shape brass: it can be hammered or rolled into sheets, drawn into rods or wire, cast in molds, forged, or pressed into dies. Its surfaces are easily worked by a variety of techniques and can be polished to a high finish. The large-scale production of brass as we know it began in Europe during the Middle Ages, particularly in Nuremberg and Flanders. It was typically hammered and worked into basins and dishes that were richly decorated by the repoussé technique or inlaid with silver (a technique particularly popular in RENAISSANCE Italy). Eighteenth-century England, particularly Birmingham and Bristol, became the center of European brass founding, with a considerable export market for brass HARDWARE AND FITTINGS and candlesticks and other LIGHTING devices. In the nineteenth century brass was sometimes given electroplated finishes.

BRONZE

Bronze, an alloy of COPPER and TIN (with copper the principal element), has been used since antiquity for utilitarian and decorative objects as well as for sculpture. Harder and more durable than copper but also malleable, ductile, and fusible, bronze can be hammered or beaten into shape or cast and then cold-worked or rolled or drawn to produce rods, wires, or sheets. Bronze resists corrosion but will weather to a lustrous brown color or develop a green film or patina. Bronze has most often been cast, usually by the lost-wax *(cire perdue)* process. A model made of wax is encased in a mold, usually of clay, and the wax is melted out. Molten bronze is then poured in, taking the place of the wax; once the metal has cooled, the mold is removed, leaving a replica of the original wax model. The bronze surface is then chased (i.e., finished with handwork) and polished.

Bronze is suitable for a number of cold-working techniques in addition to chasing, including repoussé (i.e., relief decoration) and engraved decoration. In the latter, the metal is cut away with a graving tool in linear patterns; these can be inlaid with wires of other metals and hammered down, as is done with IRON and steel. Bronze has also often been gilded, wholly or in part (the English term *ormolu* is sometimes used to describe gilt bronze). In the technique of fire- or mercury-gilding, the surface was painted with an amalgam of gold and mercury, and the object was then fired over a flame or in a low-temperature oven until the mercury volatilized, leaving a thin film of gold. The mercurous oxide fumes given off in this process were dangerous, and it was not until the nineteenth century, with improved techniques and the invention of electroplating (the process of depositing a metallic coating on a base metal in an electrolytic bath), that bronze objects could be gilded safely.

Since antiquity, bronze has also been used for luxury furnishings that were only slightly less expensive than those made of gold or silver. These included candelabra, andirons, chandeliers, furniture mounts, and other HARDWARE AND FITTINGS. Starting in the Middle Ages, separate guilds were organized in France to cast, chase, and gild bronze. By the eighteenth century, bronze craftsmen such as Pierre Gouthière and Pierre-Philippe Thomire had become celebrities with an aristocratic clientele; Thomire also designed gilt-bronze mounts for porcelains. In the nineteenth century the production of bronze household and luxury goods declined, replaced by cheaper metals, which could be given electroplated finishes or be artificially patinated to resemble bronze.

CAROLIAN—*see* RESTORATION

CARPETS

Production of carpets and rugs (the terms are interchangeable) was relatively limited in the West until the mid-nineteenth century, when power looms replaced hand manufacture and transformed carpet making into a major industry, particularly in Great Britain and the United States. Many different types of hand techniques were used for Western carpet production—flat weaving, tapestry weaving, NEEDLEWORK, and, especially in the American FOLK ART tradition, embroidering, knitting, hooking, and braiding—but knotted-pile carpets constructed with arduous and time-consuming techniques that originated in the Orient were the most prestigious. In the fabrication of

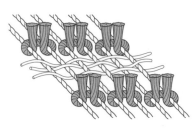

GHIORDES, OR
SYMMETRICAL, KNOT

knotted carpets, yarns of wool (or sometimes silk) are hand knotted in rows to a plain-woven foundation fabric, creating the pattern and producing a velvety pile. Except in Spain, where carpets were made with a single-warp knot, Western carpets almost exclusively used the symmetrical Turkish, or Ghiordes, knot, in which the yarn is wound around two warps, with the cut ends emerging in between.

The earliest European carpets were made in Spain, where carpet making following oriental styles was introduced under Islamic rule during the Middle Ages. By the fifteenth century, HISPANO-MORESQUE craftsmen were combining elements from the decorative traditions of Islam and Spain (armorial devices, Christian figurative motifs) and from the patterns of contemporary European silks and architectural decoration. Whereas carpets were used on floors in Spain, in northern Europe until the early eighteenth century they were more often used as table and bed coverings. During the TUDOR period, English makers copied rare and costly imported Turkish carpets (sometimes with the addition of coats of arms), such as those seen in portraits by Hans Holbein; they also created native designs with floral motifs resembling English needlework patterns, made by knotting as well as by needle. Referred to as "Turkey work" and often used for UPHOLSTERY, it continued to be produced until the late seventeenth century, when the aggressive international trade encouraged under the RESTORATION made oriental carpets plentiful and local manufacture superfluous.

The finest European carpets were those made under French royal patronage and exclusively for royal use at the Savonnerie factory in Paris, which was founded in 1627 and granted a monopoly at that time for knotted-pile carpet production in France. Its greatest achievements were the magnificent carpets woven for the Louvre between 1668 and 1689, with a BAROQUE vocabulary of acanthus, arabesques, scrolls, and royal devices that typified LOUIS XIV decoration. A center of commercial carpet production was established in 1743 at the Aubusson tapestry factory in central France, which made knotted carpets in ROCOCO floral patterns and then delicate, tapestry-woven carpets in the LOUIS XVI and EMPIRE styles. In the mid-eighteenth century, carpet knotting was reintroduced to England following French models. Thomas Moore in London supplied the carpets that Robert ADAM designed to echo his painted ceilings, while those for Thomas CHIPPENDALE's clients were generally made in the factory of Thomas Whitty in Axminster, which during the REGENCY also created the immense CHINOISERIE carpets for the Royal Pavilion at Brighton.

Machined carpets began to compete successfully with knotted ones in the eighteenth century. The English factories in Kidderminster produced a double-ply, reversible carpet in thirty-six-inch widths, joined together to create room-size floor coverings. These utilitarian products, known by the town's name, and similar ones called "Scotch" and "Ingrain" carpets, were later woven in large quantities by Jacquard looms, which could easily produce complicated patterns, and then by steam-powered looms, becoming very popular in the United States during the second half of the nineteenth century. The application of the power loom to carpet making in England in 1839 (and its introduction to America in 1841) yielded the large-scale manufacture of Brussels, Wilton, and Axminster pile carpets (named after their looms, not their places of origin). The invention of the "Spool" Axminster loom in 1876 greatly expanded the range of designs and colors, while the construction of wide, or broad, looms made possible seamless coverage of large floors.

Specialized craft production continued alongside industrial manufacture. In 1879 William Morris established his own carpet workrooms at Hammersmith in London, using flat, naturalistic ornament and Persian carpets as the inspiration for his designs (he also supplied oriental-style designs for the looms at Wilton), later manufacturing carpets in his own workshop at Merton Abbey. That same year the Friends of Finnish Handicraft was established to revive the manufacture of the traditional Scandinavian flat-pile *ryijy* rugs used as bed and bench covers. During the ART DECO period, notable rugs with geometric patterns were made in the workshop of Ivan da Silva Bruhns in Paris and at Wilton, England, after designs by Marion Dorn.

CHARLES II—*see* RESTORATION

CHARLES IX—*see* FRANCIS I

CHARLES X

▷ **WHO** CRAFTSMEN AND MANUFACTURERS: François Baudry, Pierre-Antoine Bellangé, Joseph Dufour, Grand Frères, François-Honoré-Georges Jacob-Desmalter, Jean-Baptiste-Claude Odiot, Pierre-Philippe Thomire, Jean-Jacques Werner

▷ **WHEN** 1824 to 1830

▷ **WHERE** France

▷ **WHAT** The name of Charles X, who ruled France from 1824 to 1830, is often used outside France to identify the styles that flourished during the Bourbon restoration—the reigns of Louis XVIII (1814–24) and Charles X. NEOCLASSICISM (adopted under the EMPIRE), with its revival of antique forms and ornament, continued under Charles X, becoming progressively lighter, less severe, and more decorative and emphasizing simple lines and plain surfaces. It was paralleled by the GOTHIC REVIVAL "troubador" style, which added Gothic tracery, pinnacles, and crockets to the persistent vocabulary of swans, laurel wreaths, and acanthus scrolls; these were applied to late Empire forms, however, and the results bore no relation to medieval prototypes.

Both styles appeared in the furniture and objects supplied to the crown and aristocracy and in the commercial products shown at the national trade exhibitions in Paris, much of it made by the same craftsmen and their families who had been employed by Napoleon. Originating in 1798, the trade exhibitions were held regularly by the Bourbon governments, with the firms of Grand, Dufour, Werner, and Baudry among those winning medals there. The same firms often worked in both styles; Pierre-Antoine Bellangé, for example, used the period's characteristic light-colored native woods, such as elm, inlaid with arabesques of darker woods to produce both Neoclassical and Neo-Gothic furniture.

Armchair, c. 1825–35. French. Elm inlaid with purpleheart wood, with silk upholstery (modern), 31³/₈ x 21 x 21¹/₄ in. (79.5 x 53.3 x 54 cm). Philadelphia Museum of Art; The Henry P. McIlhenny Collection in memory of Frances P. McIlhenny.

Centerpiece, 1757–59. Made in Augsburg, Germany. Silver,
height: 15¾ in. (40 cm). Museum für Kunsthandwerk, Frankfurt.

CHINOISERIE

Chinese-style, or rather what was thought to be Chinese-style, decoration—called "chinoiserie" (based on French usage)—achieved its most refined and fantastic expression during the ROCOCO period, although things oriental had fascinated Europeans ever since Marco Polo returned from the court of Kublai Khan in the thirteenth century. Imitations of imported Chinese luxury goods were immensely popular in the seventeenth century, particularly in RESTORATION England. Western craftsmen replicated the shapes and decoration of oriental wares while seeking to discover the secrets of their manufacture, especially the formulas for PORCELAIN and LACQUER. POTTERY with blue-and-white decoration, notably from the factories in Delft in Holland and Nevers in France, suggested Chinese porcelain; WALLPAPER imitated oriental painted or embroidered cloths; and colored varnishes and shellacs substituted for lacquer in a process known as "japanning." At the same time, BAROQUE follies, garden pavilions, painted and lacquered rooms, and all sorts of furnishings, fittings, and accessories were decorated in the Chinese mode.

Not until the eighteenth century, however, was the idealized imagery of chinoiserie fully defined, with its charming figures in rich flowing robes (sometimes replaced by monkeys in similar dress, called *singerie* in French) set amid landscapes with ornamental pagodas, craggy mountains, weeping willows, exotic flowers, and imaginary birds and dragons. The prestige that this genre achieved when it appeared in the work of important French artists—such as the paintings of Antoine Watteau, designs for Beauvais TAPESTRIES by François Boucher, and engravings by Jean Pillement—kept France at the center of this style as it spread throughout Europe. Chinoiserie became almost universal on the Continent and in Great Britain, appearing on some of the earliest porcelain at Meissen, French lacquer bombé commodes, and Venetian woodwork; in the celebrated teahouse (1754) of Frederick the Great at Sanssouci in Potsdam, by Johann Gottfried Büring; and on ENAMELS from Battersea in England. Much English chinoiserie, especially furniture and the silver tea paraphernalia by Paul de Lamerie, took an independent turn. New forms evolved around midcentury in the carved latticework and fretwork on chairs, sofas, screens, and beds in the Chinese CHIPPENDALE style (so-called from designs that appear in Thomas Chippendale's *Gentleman and Cabinet-Maker's Director*, 1754) and in the pagodas, canopies, mandarins, and dragons that were added as ornamentation to them.

Nineteenth-century NEOCLASSICISM supplanted large-scale chinoiserie (with the notable exception of the Chinese REGENCY decoration for the future

George IV at Carlton House in London and the Royal Pavilion at Brighton), although it continued to appear regularly in the modest lacquered TIN and PAPIER-MÂCHÉ wares of Pontypool and Birmingham and in the decorations of the ROCOCO REVIVAL. After midcentury, chinoiserie was overtaken by an interest in Japan, and Japanism became one of the central design elements of the AESTHETIC MOVEMENT.

CHIPPENDALE

▷ **WHO** Thomas Chippendale

▷ **WHEN** 1750s through 1780s

▷ **WHERE** Great Britain and America

▷ **WHAT** *Chippendale* refers to the styles of furniture illustrated in Thomas Chippendale's comprehensive design book, *The Gentleman and Cabinet-Maker's Director,* a collection of 160 plates published in 1754 and modified and enlarged in 1755 and 1762. The book made Chippendale's name a household word and did much to advance the "modern," or ROCOCO, style, although it also included Gothic and CHINOISERIE designs. By the third edition, the *Director* had been updated to include designs in which classicizing details (see NEOCLASSICISM)—legs in the form of terms, caryatids, fluted ovals, rams' heads, husks, lion masks, and picturesque classical ruins done in marquetry—were applied to forms familiar from his earlier plates. Whether "modern," Gothic, Chinese, or Neoclassical, Chippendale's designs were marked by a linear delicacy characteristic of English Rococo. His style could turn extravagant and fanciful, especially in the Rococo and Chinese modes, where serpentine toilet tables undulate on the page and temple bells bedeck a bookcase.

What made the *Director* so popular was its completeness in providing patterns for the whole range of household furniture and in giving measurements, instructions for the finish, upholstery materials, and even the intended location of individual pieces. The *Director*'s subscribers included not only the wealthy and noble but also such tradesmen as cabinetmakers, upholsterers, carpenters, and joiners. By the 1760s, copies of the *Director* reached America, where it was the most widely owned furniture design book of the eighteenth century. William Buckland in Virginia and Maryland as well as Thomas Affleck and Benjamin Randolph in Philadelphia were among the American furniture makers influenced by *Director* designs.

Ribband-Back Chairs, Plate XV from Thomas Chippendale,
"Gentleman and Cabinet-Maker's Director," London, 1755. English.
Courtesy Philadelphia Museum of Art.

Chippendale himself had a flourishing practice as a cabinetmaker and upholsterer and also as an upholder (someone able to provide the entire furnishing of a house). Despite the hundreds of items documented to have been made by his firm, comparatively few have been traced. Although countless pieces of furniture reflect the influence of his engraved designs, few are equal in quality to those that have been documented to Chippendale's own workshops.

CLOCKS

The manufacture of clocks to measure the passage of time and sometimes also to record the phases of the moon and other astronomical phenomena requires several very different crafts. The movements (with their wheels, regulating escapements, and weights or pendulums), the cases made in many different forms to enclose them, and the dials to indicate the time and give other information were often produced by separate workshops and some-times then assembled by yet other workshops or even retail establishments. Makers of the works are known from their signatures on the movements or dials (although dials can be misleading, since antique works may have been remade or replaced), but the designers of the cases, especially those made before the eighteenth century, have generally been lost in obscurity.

Early timepieces—such as the Gothic iron chamber clocks powered by weights and the RENAISSANCE spring-driven table clocks in drum shape made in southern Germany (particularly Augsburg and Nuremberg)—were not accurate and continually had to be reset. Many of the Renaissance clocks were conceived as curiosities, made by master goldsmiths in miniature archi-tectural and other decorative shapes and incorporating complex and inge-nious works that controlled delicate automata (movable figures) and auxiliary dials with astronomical and astrological indicators.

In the mid-seventeenth century, the application of Galileo's discovery of the uniform motion of the pendulum turned clocks into highly reliable timekeep-ers, and England became the most important center of precision clock mak-ing. RESTORATION clockmakers, including Thomas Tompion and Daniel Quare, refined the mechanisms of pendulum-controlled clocks and introduced a dis-tinctive, restrained style for the so-called bracket clocks, which were spring driven, as well as weight-powered standing clocks; both were made of wood and featured elaborately engraved brass dials. Architectural long-case clocks, with narrow doors opening onto the weights and pendulum, were veneered in walnut or ebony or decorated with marquetry or japanning.

English clocks were imitated in the Netherlands, Germany, Italy, Spain, and the American colonies (where in the eighteenth century Pennsylvania clockmakers established a strong tradition of creating long-case clocks) but rarely in France. French clockmakers transformed their clocks, which by convention had white-enameled dials, into interior furnishings, those in the LOUIS XIV style having ebonized wood and Boulle marquetry. Eighteenth-century bracket clocks on stands were true pieces of furniture, made by the most celebrated *ébénistes* and decorated with *vernis Martin* LACQUER, marquetry, and bronze mounts. The popular cartel (wall) clocks were given a plethora of carved and gilded ROCOCO ornament. Table and mantel clocks in bronze, which became fashionable in France toward the end of the century, were primarily decorative sculpture—small, standardized, drum-shaped timepieces set among elaborate compositions of gilding, hardstones, and porcelain figures.

Nineteenth-century American clock manufacturing was centered in New England, where Aaron Willard and Lemuel Curtis received patents in 1802 and 1816, respectively, for what later became known as banjo and girandole clocks, decorated with painting on glass and FEDERAL ornament. Clock making using standardized mechanisms fitted into cases designed in all the prevailing decorative styles became a major American industry. Manufacturers were very successful in selling great numbers of cheap, accurate instruments throughout the world, offering severe competition to makers abroad. In the 1870s the clockmakers of Germany's Black Forest region, who had flooded Europe with their cottage-industry products earlier in the century, adopted factory methods in response to the American influx and widely marketed their own popular designs—among them, the rustic, house-shaped cuckoo clock.

COLLECTIBLES—*see* ANTIQUES

COLONIAL REVIVAL

▷ **WHO** CRAFTSMEN AND MANUFACTURERS: Baker Furniture Company, Berkey & Gay Furniture Company, Gorham Company, Ferdinand Keller, Nathan Margolis, Meier & Hagen, C. F. Meislahn and Company, Wallace Nutting, Paine Furniture Company, William Savage, Sypher & Company, Seth Thomas Sons and Company, Tiffany and Company

▷ **WHEN** 1870s through 1920s

FERDINAND KELLER (established 1882).
Side Chair, 1885–1910. American. Mahogany and white pine, with
modern upholstery, height: 41 in. (104.1 cm). Dr. and Mrs. Joseph A.
Glick, Wilmington, Delaware.

(c)

▷ **WHAT** The Colonial Revival found expression in everything from paintings and popular novels to architecture and furnishings. The term *Colonial* was loosely defined, with sources in two centuries, from the JACOBEAN period of the earliest settlers to independence and, anachronistically, beyond, incorporating aspects of the late FEDERAL style (including the French-influenced American EMPIRE). Accompanying an era of revived patriotism, the Colonial Revival came of age in the decades following the nation's centennial in 1876. The style romanticized the values of the founding fathers and gave potency to earlier artifacts, such as spinning wheels and long-case clocks. The Colonial Revival embraced, above all, the ideal of simplicity and handcraftsmanship, which stood in contrast to the popular abundantly decorated, machine-made furnishings of the VICTORIAN period. Colonial Revival objects were made both by hand in small shops, such as the furniture of Ferdinand Keller of Philadelphia, and in considerably greater numbers with the aid of machines in large factories—for example, silver by Tiffany and Company, which in 1870 introduced two Colonial-style flatware patterns, Antique and Queen Anne.

Two revival crazes developed around the turn of the century: souvenir spoons decorated with American historical subjects (the majority made by the Gorham Company, of Providence, Rhode Island) and rocking chairs constructed from parts of old spinning wheels (the back was the wheel). In general, however, furniture forms approximated historical accuracy, although they might be combined in unlikely ways (such as CHIPPENDALE ball-and-claw feet on rockers), or feature a mixed and more luxuriant decorative vocabulary, or be adapted to new uses, such as Victrola cabinets and coffee tables. The pieces are lighter in weight than their original prototypes (especially those of mahogany), with flatter, cruder carving and dowel instead of mortise-and-tenon joinery (see FURNITURE).

During the second two decades of the twentieth century, which saw the first significant museum exhibitions of American furnishings and the beginning of the historic preservation movement, more historically accurate pieces were sought, typified by Tiffany's Paul Revere tea service (made about 1918 and reproduced from one in the Metropolitan Museum of Art), furniture reproductions by Baker Furniture Company (the Duncan Phyfe line of 1923), and the work of Wallace Nutting. His thorough research for books on Windsor chairs (1917), the furniture of what he called the "Pilgrim Century" (1921), and clocks (1924) culminated in Nutting's three-volume *Furniture Treasury* (1928–33), with five thousand illustrations. Applying this research to his own

(c)

furniture, Nutting made reproductions using traditional manufacturing methods, including hand turning and hand carving, thus reclaiming the craftsmanship as well as the forms and ornamentation of American antique furniture.

COMMONWEALTH—see JACOBEAN

CONDITION

The condition of an antique—that is, its current physical characteristics relative to its original state—is often a critical factor in determining its value. "Fine condition" generally assumes that the work is intact with no structural defects, with all original elements present, and retaining its original finish or surface appearance, such as the original varnish on a piece of furniture, which can be crucial to its worth. Criteria do vary from one type of object to another. Signs of ordinary use such as scratches, dents, or fine cracks, which might be considered acceptable on a piece of wooden furniture, would seriously compromise the value of a ceramic piece.

Problems in condition can result from the simple loss of parts, such as the lid from a teapot, or from mistreatment such as sharp blows, stress from changes in temperature and humidity, and exposure to sunlight, moisture, insects, airborne chemicals, and other damaging substances. These may result in warping, splitting, stains, holes, surface corrosion, and the like. Materials themselves can have inherent problems caused by their chemical composition or their manufacturing methods; for example, certain plastics or rubber products are unstable and decompose over time.

Among the most persistent threats to antiques are the attempts to restore them. This can involve the improper cleaning or stripping of surfaces, the replacement of worn parts, or the updating of old-fashioned objects in an attempt to modernize them. Such efforts to hide or disguise age or damage may result in greater alteration to the condition than was caused by the original defect. Aggressive attempts at restoration that aim to make an object appear new might destroy detail by oversanding or abrasion, cause losses of original paint by overcleaning, or weaken the structural integrity of fabrics by exposing them to harsh bleaching or cleaning agents. Careful restoration can bring an object back to a desirable condition, especially when an object is to be used, but a very different approach is taken by most museums. Their goal is to conserve or stabilize the condition of an object and to make its appearance as close to that of its original manufacture as possible, using treatments that are reversible and sometimes apparent. Misguided home remedies have been the ruin of countless antiques, and the most important factor in successfully treating an object is to begin with expert advice.

CONSERVATION—*see* CONDITION

CONSULAT—*see* EMPIRE

COPPER

The metallic element copper is reddish in color, highly malleable (easy to shape), ductile (it can be drawn into thin wires without breaking), resistant to rust, and an excellent conductor of heat, which makes it useful for cooking utensils. Copper can be worked either hot or cold; it does not crack when hammered, stamped, or forged, and it actually gains in strength when cold-hammered or cold-rolled into sheets. Yet, because of its inherent softness, copper has been most widely used in alloys with other metals: with TIN to make BRONZE, with zinc to make BRASS, and with tin, lead, and other metals to make PEWTER. Copper also combines well with GOLD AND SILVER and is the base metal from which silver plate is made.

Gilt-copper liturgical vessels were produced starting in the Middle Ages; some were decorated with ENAMELS, for which copper is the customary ground. In the sixteenth and seventeenth centuries in Germany, copper objects were also elaborately gilded, chased, engraved, and decorated with enamels and stones. But copper has more often been used for utilitarian wares, such as teapots, pans, and other cooking vessels (lined with tin to prevent the formation of soluble salts that discolor food and alter its taste), or as a substitute for more costly metals in the production of wares like snuffboxes for the middle classes in the eighteenth century. In the later nineteenth century a number of designers in the ARTS AND CRAFTS MOVEMENT in Britain and elsewhere revived the use of copper for small functional objects like candlesticks and vases and for furniture fittings.

COUNTRY

The term *country* is synonymous with *vernacular* and *common*. It has come to be applied to the simple, functional furniture and objects used by ordinary people in their homes, workplaces, and institutions. Urban as well as

Armchair, c. 1750–60. Made in Philadelphia. Painted hardwoods, 43³/4 x 25¹/4 x 18³/4 in. (III.I x 64.I x 47.6 cm). Philadelphia Museum of Art; Gift of Lydia Thompson Morris.

rural, country furniture was found in cottages, farmhouses, rowhouses, tenements, and servants' quarters, as well as inns, schools, hospitals, prisons, and churches. It was mostly the work of anonymous artisans and small workshops, which skillfully used native woods and the basic techniques of joiners and turners to create sturdy chairs, beds, tables, and cabinets in forms based on earlier and regional traditions.

In some instances country furniture also followed current high styles, but at a distance, reduced, and simplified. For example, country forms of QUEEN ANNE and LOUIS XV (see FRENCH PROVINCIAL) are clearly identifiable alongside rustic types such as Windsor chairs and trestle tables. Usually country furniture was fitted with plank, rush, or woven UPHOLSTERY; had little applied ornament (except what could be acquired ready-made, such as moldings); and was either left plain or painted with solid colors. By the nineteenth century, however, grained and decorative painted finishes became popular, especially for country pieces made of pine. *Country* is also sometimes used generally to characterize utilitarian crafts such as BASKETRY and simple objects in metal and WOOD such as kitchenwares.

CROMWELLIAN—*see* JACOBEAN

DIRECTOIRE—*see* EMPIRE, LOUIS XVI

EDWARDIAN—*see* VICTORIAN

EGYPTIAN REVIVAL—*see* EMPIRE, REGENCY

ELIZABETHAN—*see* TUDOR

EMBROIDERY—*see* NEEDLEWORK

EMPIRE

▷ **WHO** ARCHITECTS, ARTISTS, AND DESIGNERS: Jacques-Louis David, Dominique Vivant Denon, Pierre-François-Léonard Fontaine, Pierre de La Mésangère, Charles Percier

CRAFTSMEN AND MANUFACTURERS: Henri Auguste, Martin-Guillaume Biennais, Jean-François Bony, François-Honoré-Georges Jacob-Desmalter, Jean-Baptiste-Claude Odiot, Savonnerie carpet factory, Sèvres porcelain factory, Pierre-Philippe Thomire

▷ **WHEN** 1804 to 1815

▷ **WHERE** France

▷ **WHAT** The Empire style was a particularly opulent, archaeological form of NEOCLASSICISM closely identified with the tastes and political career of Napoleon I (Bonaparte). During the Directoire (1795–99), Napoleon commanded France's Army of Italy and led an important scientific and military expedition to Egypt (1798). As first consul during the Consulat (1799–1804) and as emperor (1804–15), Napoleon created an empire that covered most of western and central Europe. The style associated with his reign spread to Italy, Holland, Germany, and Spain in the wake of his military conquests and at the courts of his relatives, who became occupying rulers. After Napoleon's defeat at Waterloo in 1815, his brother Joseph Bonaparte moved to America, where his presence and his estate at Point Breeze, New Jersey, helped establish the Empire style abroad, as did the work of the émigré cabinetmaker Charles-Honoré Lannuier and silversmith Simon Chaudron (see FEDERAL).

For its decorative motifs, the Empire style used symbols of the Roman Empire (for example, laurel wreaths and eagles) and Napoleonic emblems (bees and giant *N*s), along with Egyptian architectural ornaments and motifs (hieroglyphics, sphinxes, pyramids, obelisks, winged disks, and other religious symbols), which alluded to Napoleon's successful Egyptian campaign. The latter was recorded in Dominique Vivant Denon's *Voyage dans la Basse et la Haute Egypte* (*Travels in Upper and Lower Egypt*, 1802), which had archaeologically accurate illustrations that proved a useful source for designers and craftsmen. Napoleon's official architects and designers were Charles Percier and Pierre-François-Léonard Fontaine. Their *Recueil de décorations intérieures* (1801, 1812; Collection of interior decorations) provided a manual of ornament and interior design that was highly influential in spreading the Empire style. During the Directoire they designed furniture and interiors for Josephine Bonaparte at Malmaison. During the Empire they used colossal orders, geometric forms, and strictly symmetrical arrangements to create grand public spaces in the state palaces at Saint-Cloud and the Tuileries. Percier and Fontaine designed every conceivable article of decoration, including furniture executed by the firm of François-Honoré-Georges Jacob-Desmalter incorporating boldly carved animal motifs (swans, griffins) and caryatids; carpets made by the Savonnerie factory, with brightly colored military and imperial emblems; porcelains in antique shapes made at Sèvres; and silver-gilt table services made by Martin-Guillaume Biennais.

The archaeological character of the Empire style was manifest in the revival of antique furniture forms: the X-frame Roman magistrate's seat; beds with curved head- and footboards resembling those of Roman couches; tub-shaped chairs with solid, curved (gondola) backs like Roman thrones; and tripod tables copied from prototypes found at Pompeii and Herculaneum. During the Napoleonic wars, British blockades of French ports necessitated the use in France of light-colored native woods instead of imported woods, a fashion that continued during the Bourbon restoration (see CHARLES X) and was adopted in REGENCY England.

ENAMELS

Enamels are made by fusing powdered glass to sheets of metal at high temperature, a technique known since antiquity and prized for its effect of enriching metallic objects with colored decoration. Enamels vary according to whether the metal ground is copper, bronze, gold, or silver and whether the glass mixtures contain colorants and opacifiers. Until about the eleventh century, European enamels were generally made by the cloisonné process, in which cells (or "cloisons") are created from thin strips of metal soldered onto the surface of the object to outline and contain the enamels so they do not run together during firing. From the twelfth century, the principal technique of fabrication was champlevé, in which the metal is gouged out or engraved to hold the enamel colors.

The most important center of enamel work in medieval and RENAISSANCE Europe was Limoges, situated in central France along ecclesiastical and pilgrimage routes to northern Spain and Rome. Patronized by monastic communities, Limoges produced RELIGIOUS OBJECTS such as book covers, candlesticks, incense burners, pyxes, and reliquaries, decorated with such Christian scenes as the Crucifixion and Christ in Majesty. These were sturdier and more affordable than the precious metalwares set with colored gems that were also made in this period. About 1450 at Limoges, the technique of painting enamels directly onto the surface of the object replaced the champlevé process. Using woodcuts and engravings as sources for their religious and mythological subjects, artists covered the metal ground with opaque white or black enamel then overpainted it with polychrome compositions.

Boxes, c. 1750–75. English. Enamel on copper, height of box in the shape of a woman's head: 3⅛ in. (8 cm). Philadelphia Museum of Art; Richard P. Rosenau Collection.

A number of sixteenth-century enamel-painting workshops have been documented, including those of Léonard Limosin, who worked for FRANCIS I, producing portraits and ecclesiastical as well as secular enamels, such as plates,
caskets, and saltcellars; and Pierre Reymond, who specialized in painting
enamelware in tones of black and white (grisaille). In the second half of the
eighteenth century, an important center for enamel painting flourished in
Staffordshire, England, particularly at Battersea but also at Bilston, and in
Birmingham; these rivaled the region's potteries in the production of small
objects, such as boxes and needle cases. It was there that the process of
transfer printing on enamel was introduced, in which a print is made on
paper and immediately pressed against the surface of the object, leaving
a monochrome impression like an engraving that could be overpainted
in polychrome enamels. By the nineteenth century the enamel trade had
declined, although the technique was kept alive in sporadic efforts, including
those of the French government, which created a workshop for painted
enamels at the Sèvres porcelain factory in 1845 (it closed for lack of
success in 1872), and of independent artist-enamelers like Claudius Popelin,
during the SECOND EMPIRE, and Jean Dunand, an ART DECO metalsmith and
lacquer artist.

EXPORT WARES

Export wares are products made for sale abroad, often designed to meet the
requirements of a specific foreign market. In the antiques and auction
trades, the term usually refers to decorative and useful objects made in
China (and in Japan) for the European and American markets, although the
Chinese, for example, had many trading partners and had sent porcelains to
Turkey, Arabia, and North Africa before such wares first reached Europe in
the fourteenth century. Nor was the export trade restricted to Asian factories. English potters like Wedgwood and brass founders from Birmingham
exported pottery and hardware and fittings to Europe and America in the
eighteenth and nineteenth centuries. Like Asian export wares, such English
products were usually designed for specific markets. For example, a trade
catalog advertised brass furniture mounts that could be decorated with the
French fleur-de-lis and crown, the Austrian imperial arms, or a portrait of
George Washington.

With the opening of the sea route around Africa to Asia in the late fifteenth
century, Western traders became directly active in the Far East for the first
time, oriental goods having previously been carried west by intermediaries.
The trade was dominated by Portugal in the sixteenth century, by Holland in

Hot-Water Plate, c. 1800. Chinese, made for the American market. Porcelain, height: 14½ in. (36.8 cm). Philadelphia Museum of Art; Gift of W. H. Noble, Jr.

the seventeenth century (the only Western country permitted to trade with Japan until the nineteenth century), and by England in the eighteenth century, although merchants from France, Denmark, Sweden, and other countries, including the United States from the 1780s, quickly found ports and spheres of influence in the lucrative trade. The first Chinese products to arrive in Europe were silks, gold, spices, PORCELAINS, LACQUER (in the form of screens, cabinets, and trunks), and tea. The rise of tea drinking in England in the eighteenth century spurred the importation of appropriate Chinese porcelain vessels—teapots and cups—to contain the new drink. The first porcelains exported were stock blue-and-white wares in standard Chinese shapes painted with typical floral or genre scenes, although as early as the sixteenth century there were special orders from Portugal for porcelains decorated with the royal coat of arms. By the seventeenth century the Dutch were ordering special types of tableware to conform to Western customs, supplying the Chinese with wooden models and drawn patterns to copy for saltcellars, ewers and basins, mustard pots, and the like. In the eighteenth century, at the height of the trade, furniture, paintings on glass, painted WALLPAPER, enamels, and silver were also exported to Europe. Much of the Chinese furniture was made in European, particularly English, styles but of native hardwoods, sometimes with carved decoration and brass fittings in Chinese patterns. Silver was similarly based on Western, particularly English and American, designs but could also be decorated with Chinese ornaments. During the nineteenth century the volume of exports to Europe from China and Japan declined, due to political and economic upheavals and the growth of competitive Western industries, although the trade remained strong in such specialized areas as FANS and IVORY and in commerce with America.

FANS

Fans, well known in Europe since the sixteenth century, were at first signs of status as well as useful objects. Early fans, which were fixed (or flat) and made of feathers following the model of fans brought back from the New World by Columbus, appear as prized accoutrements in many royal portraits throughout Europe. Folding fans, however, following Asian forms, soon became more commonly used. Two types were produced: pleated, in which a decorated leaf of parchment, paper, fabric, or LACE is mounted on a series of sticks, which pivot at the base to open and form a semicircular shape; and *brisé* (broken), made of sticks alone, linked at the top with a cord or ribbon and opening similarly. A variation is the cockade fan, which pivots at the top to form a completely circular fan. Sticks and "guards" (as the more elaborate

FANS

Feather Fan, 1820–30. Chinese, made for the Western market. Mount of white chicken feathers decorated with hand-painted floral design, pierced bone sticks, and metal ring, 14 x 24 in. (35.5 x 61 cm). Philadelphia Museum of Art; Gift of Mrs. Henry W. Breyer, Sr.

outer sticks are called) were made of ivory, bone, wood, mother-of-pearl, papier-mâché, or celluloid (and other early plastics), and were carved, pierced, and ornamented.

Italy was the center of European fan production for much of the seventeenth century, with France surpassing it by the beginning of the eighteenth. The broad expanses of *brisé* as well as pleated fans were settings for decoration, be it one scene covering the entire surface or several, set into painted frames and interspersed with decorative motifs. Biblical, mythological, and allegorical subjects, augmented in the eighteenth century by *fêtes galantes* (courtship scenes of elegantly dressed figures in parklike surroundings) and CHINOISERIE, were favorite themes. Less expensive and quickly printed leaves, often hand colored, could also be used to make up-to-date fans representing political and commemorative subjects, topographical views, dance steps, and popular songs. Inexpensive fans proliferated in the nineteenth century with machine manufacture and the advent of chromolithography; many were distributed as advertisements or brought back as souvenirs from, for example, the great international trade exhibitions that began in 1851. Millions of fans made as EXPORT WARES were also imported from China and, particularly in the later nineteenth century, from Japan. But the art of fan painting was also revived at this time, with Salon painters creating designs in historical styles and progressive artists such as Edgar Degas decorating fans inspired by Japan. At the end of the century, large fans (and hats) of feathers became so popular internationally that several species of exotic birds were decimated just to satisfy the demand.

FEDERAL

▷ **WHO** ARCHITECTS, ARTISTS, AND DESIGNERS: Charles Bulfinch, Thomas Jefferson, Benjamin Henry Latrobe, Pierre-Charles L'Enfant, Samuel McIntire, Charles Willson Peale, Rembrandt Peale, William Rush, William Strickland, Gilbert Stuart
CRAFTSMEN AND MANUFACTURERS: Michael Allison, Joseph B. Barry, Michel Bouvier, Simon Chaudron, Henry Connelly, Lemuel Curtis, John Davey, Simeon Deming, Daniel Dupuy, Hugh Finlay, John Finlay, John Forbes, Ephraim Haines, John Hewson, James Howell, Richard Humphreys, Charles-Honoré Lannuier, Joseph Lownes, Duncan Phyfe, Anthony G. Quervelle, Anthony Rasch, Paul Revere, Joseph Richardson Jr., Nathaniel Richardson, John Seymour, Thomas Seymour, John Shaw, Simon Willard

▷ **WHEN** 1789 through 1830s

▷ **WHERE** United States

▷ **WHAT** Federal is the name given to NEOCLASSICISM in America after the establishment of the federal system of government in 1789. Not a cohesive style, it drew inspiration from contemporary English and French forms as well as Greek and Roman antiquity. Direct classical borrowings are apparent in buildings by Thomas Jefferson and William Strickland based on ancient models (the Pantheon in Rome and the Maison Carrée in Nîmes, France); the abundant use of Roman symbols to represent the new republic (eagles, wheat sheaves, and fasces); and an ornamental vocabulary of moldings, paterae, swags, lyres, urns, and exotic creatures (dolphins, lions, sphinxes, and griffins).

The early Federal period reflected the English Neoclassicism of Robert ADAM—a light, elegant style brought to America in Adam's own *Works in Architecture* (1773–1822) as well as in the pattern books of George HEPPLE-WHITE and Thomas SHERATON. Adamesque urn and columnar shapes appear in the silver by Paul Revere in Boston and by Joseph and Nathaniel Richardson in Philadelphia. The most characteristic furniture types, borrowed from the English pattern books, included card tables, sideboards, ladies' worktables, tambour writing desks, and chairs with open oval, square, or heart-shaped backs. These were adorned with painted surfaces, carving, and mahogany veneers with inlaid ornamentation in light and dark woods. Round convex mirrors were introduced to America about the turn of the century, influencing the design of wall clocks, notably the girandole clocks by Lemuel Curtis. One Federal form, however, was particular to America, the "lolling," or (as it was later called) "Martha Washington," chair—a tall, comfortable upholstered chair with turned legs and arms.

The later Federal period relied on English REGENCY furnishings (to which the New York cabinetmaker Duncan Phyfe was partial) and the French EMPIRE style, introduced by immigrant craftsmen—among them, the silversmiths Anthony Rasch and Simon Chaudron and the furniture maker Charles-Honoré Lannuier. It also adopted the archaeology-inspired forms shown in Sheraton's *Cabinet-Maker, Upholsterer, and General Artist's Encyclopaedia* (1804–6), *Household Furniture and Interior Decoration* (1807) by Thomas Hope, and *A Collection of Designs for Household Furniture and Interior Decoration* (1808) by George Smith—splay-legged *klismos* chairs; curule, or X-shape, chairs; and Grecian couches with scrolled arms, painted and gilded or heavily carved with Greco-Roman ornament. Baltimore craftsmen specialized in painted and gilded "Grecian" furniture; a notable suite in this style

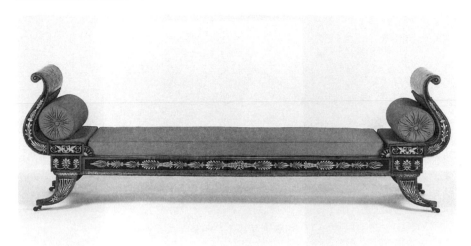

BENJAMIN HENRY LATROBE (1764–1820).

Sofa, c. 1808. American. Gessoed and painted tulipwood and maple, with gilt decoration, caning, and modern upholstery, 33¹/₂ x 103 x 23¹/₂ in. (85 x 261.6 x 59.7 cm). Philadelphia Museum of Art; Gift (by exchange) of Mrs. Alex Simpson, Jr., and A. Carson Simpson, and funds contributed by Mr. and Mrs. Robert L. Rayley and various donors.

Jointed Figure, 1860–1930. American. Painted sheet iron, iron wire, white pine, and brass, height: 31 in. (78.7 cm). Courtesy of Winterthur Museum, Winterthur, Delaware.

designed by Benjamin Henry Latrobe and decorated by John and Hugh Finlay was made for the White House in 1809.

FIGURINES—*see* STATUETTES

FOLK ART

Folk art is the work of artisans and artists distanced from mainstream society—by geography (those living in provincial regions), status (women, itinerant craftspeople, colonial populations), or belief (the Amish in Pennsylvania) —who held on to and at the same time modified traditional models, developing distinctive decorative vocabularies that demonstrated a strong sense of continuity but allowed for individual creative expression. Usually made of inexpensive local materials by hand or by simple mechanical processes, folk art was originally destined mainly for the extended community to which its maker belonged, but subsequently it often has been made for sale to outsiders as well. Many groups produced similar types of objects, but most also developed specialties that they raised to a high level of virtuosity and for which they became known: religious carvings (santos) in Mexico and the southwestern United States; sgraffito- and slip-decorated PENNSYLVANIA GERMAN redware (see POTTERY); cut paperwork in Poland; TAPESTRIES in Norway; scrimshaw, or IVORY engraved by whalers from all countries; painted oxcarts in Sicily; and NEEDLEWORK quilts in nineteenth-century America. Because such works often appear to lack sophistication, they have sometimes been regarded, mistakenly, as the creations of self-taught craftsmen, but folk objects are not necessarily less sophisticated in their conception or less well made than mainstream production. Rather, the continuity of folk art methods, forms, and motifs depends on established systems for transmission, often through instruction by relatives, schools, workshops, or apprenticeship.

Serious interest in folk art first arose in the later nineteenth century as part of the emergence of European nationalist movements, which sought to define native characteristics through the study of local history, literature, and relics from the past. Societies for the investigation and preservation of folk materials were established, leading to the founding of folk museums and to the revival of folk arts from earlier times, such as the reintroduction of *ryijy* rug making in Finland and needle LACE in Burano, Italy. Individual collecting became popular only after World War II, at the same time as the commercialization of folk forms and touristic production grew into a significant industry.

FRANCIS I

▷ **WHO** ARCHITECTS, ARTISTS, AND DESIGNERS: René Boyvin, Jean Cousin, Philibert Delorme, Jacques Androuet Du Cerceau, Jean Goujon, Pierre Lescot, Germain Pilon, Francesco Primaticcio, Rosso Fiorentino, Hugues Sambin CRAFTSMEN AND MANUFACTURERS: François Briot, Etienne Delaune, Léonard Limosin

▷ **WHEN** 1515 to 1547

▷ **WHERE** France

▷ **WHAT** The style associated with the reign of the French king Francis I (1515–47)—which continued under Henri II (1547–59), Francis II (1559–60), and Charles IX (1560–74)—was deeply influenced by the Italian RENAISSANCE. An admirer of Italian culture and the luxurious splendor of Italian court life, Francis attempted to re-create it on French soil, importing Italian architects and artists to build and decorate the royal residences. Among the Italians who worked for him were Niccolò dell' Abbate, Benvenuto Cellini, Leonardo da Vinci, Francesco Primaticcio, Rosso Fiorentino, Andrea del Sarto, and Sebastiano Serlio.

The most important of these were Francesco Primaticcio and Rosso Fiorentino, whose elegant, decorative sculpture and painting at the château of Fontainebleau (1528–40) gave the Renaissance in France and the style of Francis I their own identity. Rosso combined painted panels with a high-relief stucco framework in which tall, slender human and half-human figures were intertwined with square and circular panels, fruit garlands, and strap-work. Used throughout the stucco frame, the strapwork had the appearance of leather rolled and cut into fantastic shapes. This decorative vocabulary was adapted to other mediums when Francis supported a workshop for TAPESTRIES at Fontainebleau and the production of ENAMELS by Léonard Limosin, who was brought to court from Limoges to execute portraits along with dishes, goblets, caskets, and other wares. The fanciful, ornamental use of human figures in the strapwork at Fontainebleau inspired Hugues Sambin's pattern book of terms, human half-figures tapering into pedestals (1572), which carvers used in designing the highly sculptural two-tiered cup-boards that were introduced during this period. Italian potters established ceramics factories in Lyons and Nevers and applied the mannered decorative idiom of the period to a diversity of new forms and painted designs copied from both French and Italian engravings.

Armchair, 1550–1600. French. Walnut, height: 42 in. (112 cm). Musée du Louvre, Paris; Bequest of Baron Charles Davillier.

Armoire, 18th century, French. Oak, 96 x 53 x 22 in. (243 x 134.6 x 55.9 cm). The Metropolitan Museum of Art, New York; Gift of J. Pierpont Morgan, 1906.

Architects like Philibert Delorme traveled to Italy, and Jacques Androuet Du Cerceau and Pierre Lescot (who were inspired by Italian sources) introduced a stricter use of the classical orders—Du Cerceau being particularly influential through his engravings of grotesques, furniture, and architectural details. Du Cerceau invented architectural furniture: tables supported on piers or columns that formed an arcade under the tabletop and tall, two-stage cupboards crowned, like a building facade, with triangular or curved pediments. The *caquetoire,* a new type of chair, also appeared at this time; it had a low trapezoidal seat (wide at the front, narrow at the rear) and a back carved with architectural details, such as niches with statues.

FRENCH PROVINCIAL

French Provincial is an American term applied specifically to the decorative COUNTRY furniture *(mobilier rustique)* made for the homes of the middle-class inhabitants of the provinces of France (and Quebec). Generally the work of anonymous craftsmen, this furniture followed in simplified and often mixed forms the styles of the Parisian nobility from the RENAISSANCE to LOUIS XVI; rustic versions of LOUIS XV and LOUIS XVI continued to be created throughout the nineteenth century. Provincial furniture was less refined, using simple carved ornamentation and solid woods—turned and joined native oak, beech, fruit, and nut—rather than exotic woods, luxurious veneers, and marquetry. It varied greatly, with certain regions retaining allegiances to specific traditional forms long after the styles had run their course. Characteristic types, some developed to satisfy regional customs, include tall carved armoires with paneled double doors and grand buffets, the most spectacular topped with open shelves for the display of dishes and other tableware. Since the last century reproductions and fanciful adaptations of French Provincial furniture have been commercially produced in huge quantities.

FRENCH RENAISSANCE—*see* FRANCIS I

FURNITURE

Furniture is defined as "movable articles" that equip domestic, commercial, and public spaces. European words for furniture stress its mobile character (for example, *mobili* in Italian, *meubles* in French, and *Möbel* in German), reflecting an ancient, unsettled way of life that required furniture to be packed onto a cart as the owner moved from one dwelling to the next. Since antiquity, the construction and decoration of furniture have encouraged the development of specialized crafts. In Europe, where timber was abundant, these were largely related to woodworking and the use of hand tools until the nineteenth and twentieth centuries, when machine-produced furniture became increasingly common, using processed woods, metal, plastic, plastic laminates, and other manufactured materials.

In medieval England the activities of the woodworking trades—those of the carpenter, joiner, and turner—were regulated by guilds. Carpenters constructed wood (usually oak) furniture with boards and nails. Since the boards tended to warp and split, furniture was often secured with wrought-IRON straps and hinges for strength and stability. The blacksmiths, who provided the metal straps, developed their decorative skills to such an extent that in the thirteenth century, for example, chests and doors would be covered with rich wrought-iron scrolls and other ornaments. Boarded, or carpenter's, furniture tends to be heavy, simply constructed (often in the form of a four-cornered box), and limited in size by the maximum width of the planks used.

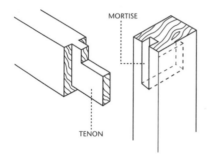

MORTISE

TENON

JOINTS: MORTISE AND TENON

Joiners carved and fit pieces of wood together to make furniture and paneling. In fourteenth-century Flanders, joiners first overcame the drawbacks of carpenter's furniture by constructing furniture with framed panels—the horizontal members known as "rails," the main vertical members as "stiles." In panel construction, thin boards or panels are set within grooved frames, where they are free to move and shrink more freely (preventing the wood from warping and splitting) even though they are held in place with mortise-and-tenon joints. In such joints, the oldest and most basic form of joining wooden parts, a projection (or "tenon") on one piece fits exactly into a slot (or "mortise") of corresponding size in the other and sometimes is secured by dowels or pegs. This structural technique demands accuracy in making the joint and skill in smoothing the surfaces. When constructing boxes or drawers instead of frames, joiners would use dovetail joints with fan-shaped (or "dove") tails and corresponding slots that closely interlock at right angles and sometimes are fixed with glue.

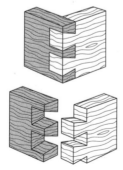

JOINTS: DOVETAIL

Panel construction could be used for only a limited range of furniture forms—chests, chairs in boxlike

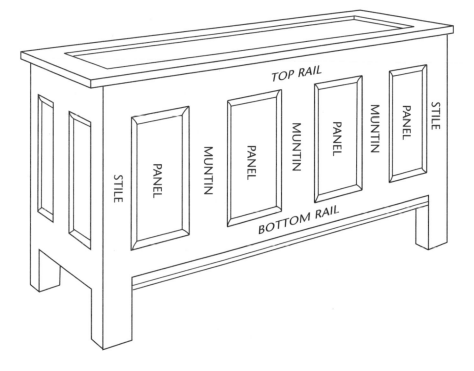

PANEL CONSTRUCTION

form, cupboards, and similar enclosed pieces, such as headboards, that could be made from flat areas of paneling. During the RENAISSANCE in northern Europe, it was also used for wall paneling (called "wainscot" in TUDOR England). In the fifteenth century the panels were typically decorated with carved patterns resembling folds of cloth known as "linenfold"; carved portrait medallions and sculptural subjects in antique styles gradually replaced linenfold decoration in the sixteenth century.

Turners made furniture by shaping pieces of wood with chisels while the wood revolved on a lathe and then fitting them together with a simple, round version of the mortise-and-tenon joint. Producers of decorative spindles as well as of varied WOOD items—including spinning wheels, carriage wheels, cups, bowls, dishes, tool handles, buttons, and boxes—turners were normally considered decorators of joined furniture. According to English guild regulations, they were not permitted to make joints or to use glue like the joiners or nails like the carpenters. During the RESTORATION in the seventeenth century, English turners made furniture that flaunted a particular exuberance, such as chairs with multiple turned uprights. Turned chairs were exported to and made in colonial America (particularly New England) and collected and revived during the nineteenth-century Elizabethan Revival and the COLONIAL REVIVAL.

In France during the late seventeenth and eighteenth centuries, richly elaborate furniture was required for Versailles and the other royal residences of LOUIS XIV, LOUIS XV, and LOUIS XVI, and the furniture-making guilds developed exceptional, specialized skills to meet the demand. The joiner (or *menuisier*) worked solid wood to construct seat furniture and case pieces (such as cupboards), of walnut, beech, and increasingly in the later eighteenth century, imported mahogany. The *menuisier* collaborated with a woodcarver or sculptor, who provided relief decoration (such as the festoons of flowers, shells, and latticework popular under Louis XIV and the RÉGENCE), and with a painter, gilder, or dyer, who colored, gilded, or tinted the woods to produce realistic and brilliant effects. To protect the surface of the wood from dirt and abrasion, to keep the colors from fading, to impede expansion and contraction, and to enhance a piece's general appearance, finishes or transparent coatings were applied to the surface after it was carefully prepared. Finally, the upholsterer provided soft furnishings for seats and beds.

In the seventeenth century *menuisiers* developed the art of veneering, or decorating the furniture with thin sheets of rare woods or other materials. When composed of shaped pieces and arranged in patterns, decorative veneers are referred to as "marquetry"; for example, marquetries of leaves

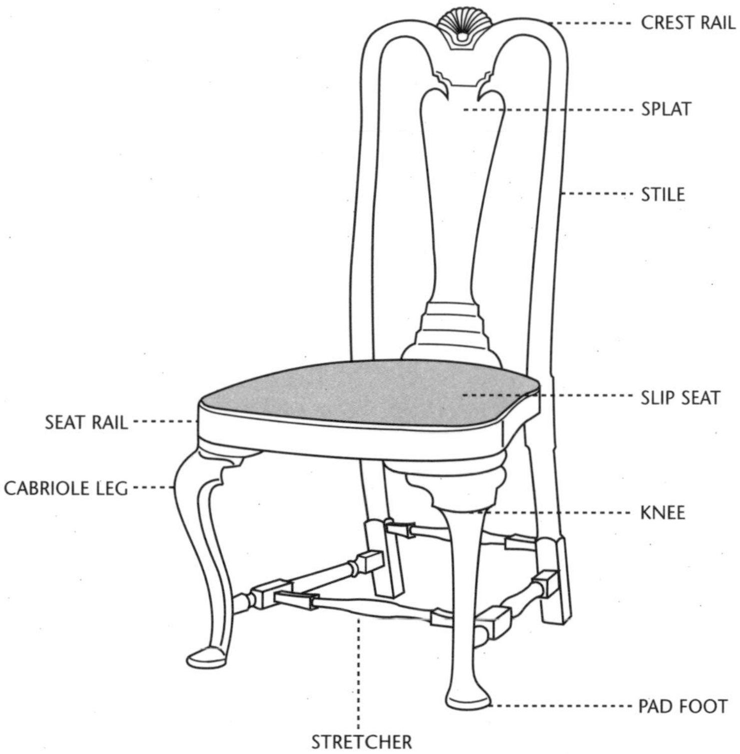

CREST RAIL

SPLAT

STILE

SLIP SEAT

SEAT RAIL

CABRIOLE LEG

KNEE

PAD FOOT

STRETCHER

PARTS OF A CHAIR

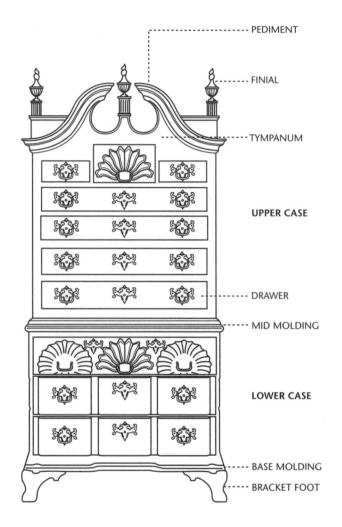

PEDIMENT

FINIAL

TYMPANUM

UPPER CASE

DRAWER

MID MOLDING

LOWER CASE

BASE MOLDING

BRACKET FOOT

PARTS OF A CASE PIECE

and flowers were created by Dutch and French makers in the seventeenth century. Most famous of these was André-Charles Boulle, who so popularized marquetries of tortoiseshell and brass that they have been identified with his name ever since. Those parts of Boulle's furniture not decorated with marquetry were generally veneered with ebony, and the use of ebony became so widespread that craftsmen who worked in ebony were distinguished as a separate category and called *menuisiers en ébène,* or *ébénistes.* The *ébénistes* were primarily makers of cabinets (first in ebony but later also with inlays of different woods and of shell, ivory, copper, pewter, bronze, silver, marble, and hardstones) and the associated term *cabinetmaker* has remained in English usage. In the eighteenth century the cabinetmaker's craft was differentiated from that of the traditional *menuisiers,* who worked largely on chairs and other simple, coarse furniture.

For the gilt-bronze mounts and HARDWARE AND FITTINGS that decorated their furniture and protected the more vulnerable parts of the marquetry, *ébénistes* collaborated with two metalworking guilds, the bronze founders and the gilders. The founders *(fondeurs-ciseleurs)* cast and chased the bronze; the gilders *(ciseleurs-doreurs)* gilded it. The task of coordinating the work of the various craftsmen who belonged to different guilds in France often fell to the dealers *(marchands-merciers).* The *marchands-merciers* are credited with inventing new combinations of materials and techniques, such as the use of decorative porcelain plaques on furniture beginning in the 1760s.

The extraordinary craftsmanship and splendid appearance of the best eighteenth-century furniture—made not only in France, which led European fashion, but also elsewhere in Europe and in Great Britain and America—guaranteed the high esteem in which it has since continuously been held. In the nineteenth century (see VICTORIAN and SECOND EMPIRE), revivals of eighteenth-century and earlier styles and techniques were aided by machines that lowered costs and made even quite elaborate furniture more widely available. Power-driven saws, for example, enabled faster and more precise sawing and shaping of wooden boards and slicing of veneers. Even the production of wicker and cane furniture, traditionally handmade by BASKETRY techniques, became partly industrialized in the mid-nineteenth century.

The advent of machine tools also brought new manufactured materials, new methods of construction, and styles that often expressed their mechanical origins. In Austria the furniture maker Michael Thonet pioneered the bending of solid and laminated lengths of beechwood, made malleable by steam, to form curved rods that were assembled into "bentwood" furniture. Mass-produced and lacking any ornament other than the flowing curves and loops produced by steam-bending, Thonet's bentwood furniture has been seen in the twentieth century as a forerunner of MODERNISM. In the United States, John Henry Belter also experimented with laminated woods, which he bent with steam in intricately curved molds and combined with solid pieces to create opulent ROCOCO REVIVAL furniture. Other new processed materials included PAPIER-MÂCHÉ (made at midcentury with improved pressing and molding machines) and metal (in the form of cast iron, wire, or hollow metal tubing), used largely in garden and hall furniture. In the 1920s the widely imitated tubular-steel furniture developed by the Hungarian-born designer Marcel Breuer brought metal furniture into domestic use, challenging traditional wood construction. Steel was viewed by progressives in France and Germany as a modern material, typical of industrialization and thus considered more suitable for the contemporary household than the luxury furniture that a number of ART DECO firms were still making by hand (and machine) with rare and costly woods in the grand tradition of eighteenth-century cabinetmaking.

GEORGIAN

▷ **WHO** ARCHITECTS, ARTISTS, AND DESIGNERS: Robert Adam; Richard Boyle, third Earl of Burlington; William Chambers; Thomas Chippendale; Hubert-François (Bourguignon) Gravelot; George Hepplewhite; Henry Holland; Thomas Johnson; William Kent; Batty Langley; Thomas Langley; Matthias Lock; John Nash; Louis-François Roubiliac; Thomas Sheraton; John Soane; James "Athenian" Stuart; John Vardy
CRAFTSMEN AND MANUFACTURERS: Matthew Boulton, Bow porcelain factory, Chelsea porcelain factory, John Cobb, Paul Crespin, Derby porcelain factory, William Ince, Paul de Lamerie, Pierre Langlois, John Linnell, John Mayhew, Nicholas Sprimont, William Vile, Josiah Wedgwood, George Wickes, David Willaume, Worcester porcelain factory

▷ **WHEN** 1714 to 1811

▷ **WHERE** Great Britain

▷ **WHAT** The term *Georgian* is applied to the varied styles of architecture and decorative arts that flourished in Great Britain during the reigns of George I (1714–27), George II (1727–60), and George III (1760–1820) until the REGENCY (1811–1820), but sometimes also includes the reign of George IV (1820–30).

Throughout the eighteenth century, these styles were greatly influenced by ideas from continental Europe. Under George I, Lord Burlington and William Kent introduced a classical style drawn from the work of the Italian RENAISSANCE architect Andrea Palladio (and the English architect Inigo Jones) and from Italian BAROQUE ornament. British "Palladian" buildings were planned symmetrically and proportionally, with pedimented facades articulated by the classical orders. The decoration of interiors and furniture was heavily sculptural, with fat acanthus leaves, scallop shells, classical figures, putti, and animals. Kent was one of the first English architects to create complete, unified interiors, designing highly architectural furniture—such as the huge pier glasses and tables and monumental seating with shell decoration for Houghton Hall, Norfolk (1731), the shells echoing the plasterwork ceilings there.

In the 1730s, under George II, Palladian classicism was gradually superseded by the new modern French ROCOCO style, which abandoned regular forms for asymmetry, serpentine lines, and light, elegant scroll- and shellwork ornament. Rococo was spread by French and Huguenot artists and craftsmen working in London (among them Paul Crespin, Gravelot, Paul de Lamerie, Nicholas Sprimont, and the sculptor Louis-François Roubiliac), as well as by pattern books and engravings; it was developed by native craftsmen and designers such as Matthias Lock, Thomas Johnson, Thomas CHIPPENDALE, and George Wickes. French forms and practices were adopted throughout the decorative arts. Chair frames and splats were carved in increasingly intricate serpentine forms, console tables were fixed to the wall, case pieces were enriched with metal inlays and mounts, and "commodes" (chests of drawers) introduced. Silverwares, by de Lamerie and others, adapted designs by such French artists as Just-Aurèle Meissonnier; textile designs emphasized naturalistic floral motifs along with a Rococo vocabulary of C-scrolls, shells, and asymmetrical cartouches; and the porcelains made at Bow, Worcester, and Chelsea copied French (as well as German) models.

By about 1760, with George III, a return to the "true" classical style of architecture, furnishings, and decoration was under way, advanced by James "Athenian" Stuart, William Chambers, and Robert ADAM. They brought back from their trips to Greece and Italy a specifically archaeological approach to antiquity, which became influential through their work and their detailed publications of classical monuments (see NEOCLASSICISM). Those publications provided repertories of Neoclassical motifs—anthemion, patera, tripod urn, and winged griffin—that were widely adopted by other architects and designers and by painters, carvers, stucco workers, embroiderers, tapestry weavers, and cabinetmakers. Some of Chambers's and Adam's designs were used in gilt-bronze objects by Matthew Boulton, ceramic figures by Josiah Wedgwood, and furniture by Chippendale, John Linnell, and Ince and Mayhew.

Neoclassical pattern books by Adam, George HEPPLEWHITE, and Thomas SHERA-TON, along with Rococo ones by Chippendale, Johnson, and Lock, helped spread Georgian styles in America. By the 1790s the delicacy and refinement that generally characterized these designs had already lost favor in Britain to the REGENCY's more massive and grandly scaled form of Neoclassicism.

GLASS

Glass is a hard, translucent, and often transparent material made largely of sand (silica), soda (sodium), and lime (calcium oxide), which are heated and fused. If nothing is added to the mixture, the glass is usually tinted bluish green by the iron in the sand. Glass can be colored by adding metallic oxides, such as copper for red, cobalt for deep blue, and manganese for yellow or purple. In its molten state, glass can be formed in a mold or shaped with tools and decorated while gathered at the end of a rod or blowpipe; after it has cooled and hardened, it also can be shaped and deco-ration can be added by various cold techniques such as engraving or cutting.

Early glasswares in Europe and the Near East were typically decorated with gold, enamel, glass threads, and appliqués. The production of thin, colorless *cristallo* in Venice during the sixteenth century created an aesthetic ideal that was widely imitated in glasshouses throughout Europe. Almost weight-less, this new material allowed glassmakers to blow and manipulate elegant, fanciful forms with intricate pincered details. Since it was clear and rela-tively free of bubbles and impurities, *cristallo* could also be decorated by the then new technique of engraving with a handheld diamond point, which set off its brilliance and transparency.

The invention of lead glass in England during the seventeenth century, achieved by adding lead oxide to the mix, produced a strong, heavy glass that was even clearer and "whiter" than *cristallo;* it became the favored medium for table glass there and in the Netherlands, to which it was exported. Lead glass was thick enough to permit deep wheel-engraved deco-ration. The technique of cutting glass on the wheel was perfected in the sev-enteenth and eighteenth centuries by Bohemian and German glass engravers, who used it to produce dense, complicated patterns and scenes.

Claret Jugs, c. 1810. Made in Warrington, England. Cut glass, height: 13¹/₂ in. (34 cm). Mallett, London.

In the later eighteenth century, British and Irish factories developed a decorative style of deep geometrical cutting on clear lead glass that achieved international popularity in the early nineteenth century, when such cut glass was copied by French, Belgian, and American factories; its popularity has survived to the present day. Nineteenth-century cut glasses were typically simpler in design, with broad concave and convex facets; in BIEDERMEIER Vienna, such glasses were painted with miniature scenes, while in Bohemia they were produced in a variety of rich, deep colors.

By the mid-nineteenth century, however, cut glass had fallen temporarily out of favor, partly due to the appearance on the market of inexpensive pressed-glass imitations produced by machines developed in America in the 1820s and later used in European factories. Glass pressing produced ornamental and table glass, often in sets with a single pattern, in huge quantities and at remarkable speeds, which superseded the practice of blowing glass into molds (except for commercial bottle making).

In reaction, many glassmakers sought inspiration in historical techniques. For example, Venetian furnace-formed constructions of the sixteenth century were revived by Venetian factories and others, as was Roman cameo glass. At the end of the century, artist-glassmakers like the American Louis Comfort Tiffany reproduced with metallic oxides the colorful iridescence that centuries of burial had given ancient glass. In the first decades of the twentieth century, artists such as the French glassmaker Maurice Marinot, using a broad range of materials and techniques, created original experimental glass independent of the increasingly industrialized commercial glass factories.

GLAZE—*see* PORCELAIN, POTTERY

GOLD AND SILVER

Gold and silver are metallic elements valued since antiquity for their rarity and beauty; to this day their possession is considered a mark of wealth. Yellow in color, gold is soft, ductile (it can be drawn out into fine wire), malleable (it can be hammered into thin sheets), and resistant to chemicals and rust. Silver is lustrous gray in color, harder than gold but also ductile and malleable, and also resistant to many chemicals. However, exposure to sulfur compounds in the air and chlorine compounds in table salt, food, and other products causes silver to tarnish, or turn black.

Both gold and silver are generally too soft to be made into useful objects in their pure states and must be combined with some other metal in an alloy. Gold is usually alloyed with copper or silver; the alloys are measured in carats, or units of one twenty-fourth, pure gold being twenty-four carat. Silver is usually mixed with copper, the proportions of the alloy varying according to country and period; in England the alloy was standardized as "sterling" at 925 parts silver per 1,000 (except for a short period between 1697 and 1720). In order to ensure the proper quantity of alloy, to maintain uniform standards, and to protect the public against inferior metal, official marks (see MARKS, SIGNATURES, AND LABELS) have been applied to gold and silver wares since the Middle Ages (as well as in antiquity). Since 1300, for example, a leopard's head stamp has been used by the assay office in London to mark sterling silver.

In 1742 Thomas Boulsover of Sheffield, England, discovered a method of "plating," or fusing, sterling silver to copper and then rolling it into sheet. Sometimes called "Sheffield plate," this plated silver was less costly than solid sterling but more liable to wear (the copper eventually shows through). It was rarely marked, although Matthew Boulton, the first successful producer of silver-plated domestic wares, did mark his work, with two suns. In 1840 G. R. Elkington patented the process of electroplating, which largely superseded Sheffield plating as a method of coating objects with silver. Electroplating deposits a skin of silver (or gold) on a finished base-metal article (often of nickel, although sometimes copper or bronze) by passing an electric current through a solution containing pure silver (or gold). Before the nineteenth century, the technique of mercury-gilding (see BRONZE) was used to coat silver, bronze, and other metals with gold.

Whether using silver, gold, or plate, silversmiths and goldsmiths raise useful and decorative objects from flat sheets by hammering them to the required shape. Variations on hammering—forging over an anvil or beating out a shape over a groove—are traditional techniques used for cutlery. Since the nineteenth century, silverware has also been produced by mechanically stamping the metal against dies—a less expensive, if less individual, process than raising them by hand. Some small articles, as well as handles, spouts, and feet for hollow ware, are made by casting molten metal in a mold. Gold and silver wares can also be decorated by the addition of solid cast ornaments, thin pieces of metal, wire moldings, openwork panels (filigree), ENAMELS, or appliqués of stones and other materials.

Decorations are also produced by "chasing" (finishing the surface of the metal) as well as by cutting away the metal with piercing and engraving. In addition, patterns in low relief can be created with variously shaped punches. The use of punches to raise relief patterns from the back is called "repoussé work": domed punches produce curved shapes ("bosses") in a repoussé technique know as "embossing." The bosses can be given additional detail and definition by chasing them from the front. Designs can also be scratched or engraved into the metal with gravers or other tools, or pierced, using hammer and chisel (or since the late eighteenth century, a piercing saw), producing very delicate and intricate linear patterns. Since the nine-teenth century, patterns have also been etched with acid, a technique not typically associated with hand-raised wares.

The styles and techniques of fashioning and decorating gold and silver wares have varied greatly over the centuries, and multiple methods have often been combined in a single piece. The publication of printed pattern books in the RENAISSANCE, for example, popularized engraved decorations, which were used with embossed patterns of naturalistic foliage, sprays of fruit, and the like. BAROQUE goldsmiths fashioned heavily embossed plate, often with sculp-tural cast handles, whereas QUEEN ANNE wares were notably simple, with little embossed or engraved decoration, relying for their effect on shape, surface reflections, and the pattern of the hammer on unadorned metal. Many his-torical gold and silver wares have not survived. Made to display the wealth as well as the taste of the owner, they were often melted down and con-verted to cash in times of financial difficulties—most famously in the case of the solid silver suite of furniture created at vast expense for the state apart-ments of LOUIS XIV at Versailles, which was melted down in 1689 to finance the costs of the king's wars.

GOTHIC REVIVAL

▷ **WHO** ARCHITECTS AND DESIGNERS: William Beckford, Richard Bentley, William Burges, William Butterfield, Alexander Jackson Davis, William Halfpenny, Batty Langley, William Morris, A. C. Pugin, A. W. N. Pugin, J. P. Seddon, Bruce J. Talbert, Eugène-Emmanuel Viollet-le-Duc, Horace Walpole, Philip Webb, James Wyatt
CRAFTSMEN AND MANUFACTURERS: Thomas-Joseph Armand-Calliat, Charles Meigh, Placide Poussielgue-Rusand, Wenzel Till
THEORIST: John Ruskin

▷ **WHEN** 1750s through 1870s

▷ **WHERE** Europe and the United States

$$\textcircled{G}$$

▷ **WHAT** The Gothic Revival, or Neo-Gothic, drew inspiration from the architecture, design, and ornament of the European Gothic styles of the twelfth through the fifteenth century. Characteristic Gothic architectural forms—pointed arches, geometric tracery, columnar construction, and ribbed vaulting—were applied to all manner of buildings and useful objects, often fancifully, without regard for the scale or function of the medieval precedent. By incorporating ornamental details such as traceried arches, pinnacles, and crockets in metalwork, pottery, furniture, stained glass, and the like, designers achieved the formal effects of intricacy and variety, and the association with the distant past, that made the Neo-Gothic style a romantic alternative to the orderly rationalism of NEOCLASSICISM. Its proponents in the eighteenth century identified "Gothic" as picturesque and stressed its sentimental properties, while in the nineteenth century, under such reformers as A. W. N. Pugin and John Ruskin in England, Gothic acquired Christian and moral overtones because of its ecclesiastical origins and "honest" structure and craftsmanship.

The Gothic Revival flourished from the mid-eighteenth century, particularly in England, where it was used first in garden buildings (the Gothic "ruin" at Hagley, Worcestershire, 1748) and later for interiors, often combined or associated with CHINOISERIE. Demonstrating the possibilities of Gothic for modern domestic architecture and interiors were Horace Walpole's Strawberry Hill (from about 1750) in Twickenham, Middlesex, the first house in the Gothic Revival style, and William Beckford's Fonthill Abbey (from 1796) in Wiltshire, built by James Wyatt. Furniture makers and designers catered to the new fashion, among them Thomas CHIPPENDALE, whose *Gentleman and Cabinet-Maker's Director* (1754) included designs in the Gothic style. The romantic taste for Gothic was encouraged in England during the REGENCY period by the best-selling novels of Sir Walter Scott and in France by the young Honoré de Balzac and Victor Hugo, who wrote novels with medieval settings during the CHARLES X and LOUIS-PHILIPPE periods. The nineteenth century saw an increasingly archaeological approach to the style, particularly in the work of A. W. N. Pugin, whose designs were close to medieval models (unlike the popular wares of Charles Meigh and other firms), and through the influence of the Ecclesiological Society, an association of architects and writers (established 1839). Ruskin's writings (*The Seven Lamps of Architecture*, 1849; *The Stones of Venice*, 1851–53) added a new social dimension to Gothic Revival theory, stressing the authenticity and morality of objects executed in their entirety by a single craftsman and rejecting modern industrial specialization and division of labor. Ruskin's ideas were taken up by the protagonists of the ARTS AND CRAFTS MOVEMENT, led by William Morris. The first examples of furniture by Morris's firm (designed by Philip Webb) were shown in the Medieval Court at the London International Exhibition of 1862.

Unlike Neoclassicism, Gothic Revival was viewed as a national style with historical and patriotic associations. All over Europe, nineteenth-century architects and designers rediscovered Gothic, although their efforts were often concentrated on the restoration or preservation of Gothic buildings, such as Eugène-Emmanuel Viollet-le-Duc's work in France at Notre-Dame, Paris (from 1845), Carcassonne (from 1852), and the château of Pierrefonds (from 1858), the latter including some original designs for Neo-Gothic furniture and decorations. For old and new churches in France and abroad, the French silversmiths Thomas-Joseph Armand-Calliat and Placide Poussielgue-Rusand supplied metalwork for RELIGIOUS OBJECTS in medieval styles. In Germany, Gothic was identified as the "Old German" *(altdeutscher)* style and adapted to buildings as various as Neuschwanstein, the castle built for Ludwig II of Bavaria (from 1869), and the new city hall in Munich (from 1867), built in a Flemish Gothic idiom by the architect Georg von Hauberrisser and furnished with German Gothic Revival furniture made after his designs by the firm of Wenzel Till. Ludwig II wrote to the composer Richard Wagner that he was "rebuilding" Neuschwanstein "in the genuine style of the old German knights' castles"; with a minstrels' hall like that in Wagner's *Tannhäuser,* dark woodwork, tapestries, and a canopied bed decorated with tiny Gothic spires, Neuschwanstein was a romantic shrine to the age of German chivalry.

The Gothic Revival flourished in America during the 1840s and 1850s, advanced by Alexander Jackson Davis, who built the house now known as Lyndhurst near Tarrytown, New York, in 1841 and designed furniture in the Gothic style for it. Although the dominant taste of America at midcentury was ROCOCO REVIVAL, Davis's associate, A. J. Downing, in his widely circulated book, *The Architecture of Country Houses* (1850), advocated the use of the Gothic style for libraries, halls, and bedrooms.

GREEK REVIVAL—*see* FEDERAL, NEOCLASSICISM, REGENCY

HALLMARKS—*see* MARKS, SIGNATURES, AND LABELS

HARDSTONES

Hardstones, known in Italian as *pietre dure*, are rare and semiprecious stones composed largely of silicates; they include agates, alabaster, amethyst, carnelian, chalcedony, jade, jasper, lapis lazuli, malachite, obsidian, onyx, porphyry, and topaz. Because of their hardness, they are worked with small saws, metal wires, and other such incisive instruments. The practice and techniques of working hardstones, developed in antiquity for decorative luxury objects and small sculptures, were revived during the RENAISSANCE by Italian craftsmen at the courts of Florence, Naples, Madrid, Prague, Paris, and elsewhere. The first workshop for hardstones, the Opificio delle Pietre Dure, was founded in Florence in 1588 under the patronage of Ferdinand I de' Medici and continues to the present as a center for their restoration.

Standing cups, ewers, large vases, and the like were carved out of hardstones and set in gold, silver, and enamel mounts for court treasuries as objects of high value and virtuoso technique. From the later sixteenth century, pictorial MOSAICS of these colorful stones—arranged to represent naturalistic flowers, landscapes, and even figural scenes—were used to decorate cabinets, tabletops, and other pieces of furniture. This practice continued well into the nineteenth century, when machine techniques contributed to the ease and virtuosity of production. Machine techniques also expanded the use of hardstones on a large scale in the nineteenth century, notably for malachite, which was used in Russia for ornamental columns and the like.

HARDWARE AND FITTINGS

Hardware and fittings in BRASS, BRONZE, COPPER, IRON, and steel were supplied by metalworkers to housebuilders, upholsterers, and furniture makers to protect and embellish various domestic articles and to make them functional. A brass founder, for example, might produce knockers, bolts, handles, knobs, doorplates, hinges, and latches for doors; rods and rings for curtains; hooks, rings, and nails for frames; hooks, knobs, and ornaments for chimneypieces and fenders; and candelabra, sconces, candlesticks, sockets and pans, and chains for lamps. In addition, the founder would produce decorative and functional fittings for FURNITURE, including drawer handles, knobs, key escutcheons, locks, bolts, hinges, casters, and feet. By the eighteenth century, metalworkers regularly published trade catalogs, which were largely anonymous (the names of the manufacturers were deliberately concealed by the agents who sold the designs to their customers). Certain eighteenth-century furniture designers, Robert ADAM among them, included decorative fittings in their published designs, which influenced the commercial trade.

Most of the hardware and fittings that survive have been made by the traditional processes of beating, rolling, casting, or stamping, and finished simply by polishing and lacquering. Only the best and most expensive furniture mounts were elaborately chased and gilded in workshops that supplied such leading cabinetmakers as Thomas CHIPPENDALE. In France, where chasers and gilders had their own guilds, Pierre Gouthière and other such craftsmen were famous, Gouthière providing members of the courts of LOUIS XV and LOUIS XVI with costly gilt-bronze fittings for chimneypieces, doors, looking-glass frames, chandeliers, and carriages. From the mid-nineteenth century, GOLD AND SILVER surfaces were produced on hardware and fittings by electroplating, an inexpensive industrial technique. In the late nineteenth and early twentieth centuries, certain ARTS AND CRAFTS MOVEMENT and ART NOUVEAU designers revived the use of handmade iron and copper furniture fittings, following medieval precedents if not styles, with cabinets, chests, and cupboards of vaguely Gothic form fitted with ornamental straps, hinges, and lockplates in floral and geometric styles.

HENRI II—*see* FRANCIS I

HEPPLEWHITE

▷ **WHO** George Hepplewhite

▷ **WHEN** 1780s to early 1800s

▷ **WHERE** Great Britain

▷ **WHAT** The Hepplewhite style derives from the some three hundred designs for "every article of household furniture" published by the widow of the cabinetmaker George Hepplewhite in *The Cabinet-Maker and Upholsterer's Guide* (1788, with revised editions in 1789 and 1794). No actual work can be attributed to Hepplewhite, and it is not even known if the simple, graceful, and utilitarian furniture shown in the plates represents his own designs. Hepplewhite furniture mirrored the broad taste for NEOCLASSICISM in England during the last quarter of the eighteenth century, particularly as interpreted by Robert ADAM. Most closely associated with Hepplewhite are chairs with shield-, oval-, and heart-shaped backs (which were not original with him) and ornamentation of wheat ears and the Prince of Wales's feathers (which

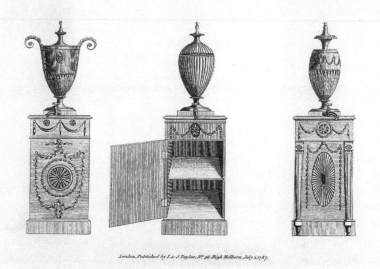

Plate 35 from George Hepplewhite, "The Cabinet-Maker and Upholsterer's Guide," London, 1794. Philadelphia Museum of Art Library.

may have been). The *Guide* emphasizes coloristic effects and decoration: chests and tables of light, shimmering satinwood inlaid with scrolls, urns, ribbons, acanthus, and other antique motifs; and chairs either of carved mahogany or finished "with painted or japanned work, which gives a rich and splendid appearance to the minuter parts of the ornaments." Hepplewhite designs, and those by his contemporary Thomas SHERATON, were the foundation for the REGENCY style in England, and their instructive pattern books also gave guidance and inspiration to the provincial cabinetmakers who created the FEDERAL style in America.

HISPANO-MORESQUE

▷ **WHEN** 1300s through 1500s

▷ **WHERE** Spain

▷ **WHAT** The arts fusing Spanish and Muslim traditions that were created in Spain during and after Islamic rule are loosely called Hispano-Moresque. The term has been applied to architecture, CARPETS, ivory, metalwork, silks, and wood carving, but it is most specifically connected with the ceramic lusterware industry that developed principally in Malaga in the thirteenth century. Lusterware—POTTERY fired with an iridescent metallic surface—probably came with Muslim craftsmen from Persia or Fatimid Egypt. It reached an outstanding level in the late fourteenth century during the Nasrid period, particularly with a series of monumental jars ornamented with the geometric figures, plant motifs, arabesques, and Kufic script that are associated with the contemporary Alhambra palace in Granada.

As Islamic power waned, the production of lusterware, which had become known as "Malaga work" *(obra de malica),* shifted to the town of Manises in Christian Valencia. The ceramics of Manises were at first indistinguishable from Malaga's but then developed a distinctive compact amalgam of late Gothic European figurative forms and stylized Islamic plant forms, six-pointed stars, Arabic lettering (which later became purely decorative), and symbolic imagery, which was used to embellish traditional Iberian pottery and TILES. An allover design of leafy bryony-gourd vines in alternating blue and copper luster was among the often-used patterns decorating the pieces later exported throughout Europe and frequently shown in Renaissance paintings. Pottery in imitation of Hispano-Moresque *obra de malica* work was made in Italy in the fifteenth century and called "majolica"—a name that then came to be applied to any tin-glazed earthenware (see POTTERY), with or

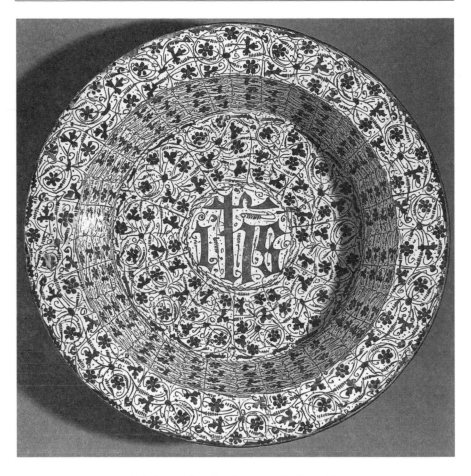

Dish (brasero), mid-15th century. Made in Valencia, Spain. Earthenware, with blue and copper luster decoration, diameter: 18⁷/₈ in. (48 cm). J. Paul Getty Museum, Los Angeles.

without luster decoration. In the nineteenth century, the techniques of Hispano-Moresque lusterware were revived in England, notably in the tiles, vases, and plates by the potter William De Morgan.

INTERNATIONAL STYLE—*see* MODERNISM

IRON

Iron has been used principally for utilitarian products. Silvery white in its pure state, iron is malleable (easy to shape), ductile (able to be drawn into thin wires without breaking), and combines easily with other elements, such as oxygen (to form iron oxide or rust) and carbon (to make steel). Because of its hardness and strength, iron has been used since antiquity for weapons, tools, and HARDWARE AND FITTINGS (as has steel, which is tougher than iron and keeps its edge, but which was rarely used before the eighteenth century). Iron is produced from ores or mixtures of materials and refined under heat in a furnace. Iron with a low carbon content (and containing impurities, such as silica) is known as "wrought iron"; it is fibrous, soft, and easy to hammer at white heat. Iron with a high carbon content is known as "cast iron." It has been produced since the sixteenth century in Europe in blast furnaces, in which the iron is melted out of its ores and is run off, or cast, into molds. In the eighteenth century, when charcoal, the traditional furnace fuel, was superseded by coke, blast furnaces could operate at higher temperatures and render the iron more fluid, so that it could be cast in finer, more delicate molds. Less expensive to produce, cast iron gradually replaced wrought iron in the nineteenth century, although wrought iron returned to favor among artist-craftsmen of the ARTS AND CRAFTS MOVEMENT and the ART NOUVEAU and ART DECO periods. From antiquity, wrought-iron tools, weapons, and hardware were often elaborately decorated, particularly with an inlay, or damascening, process (named after Damascus, where it was perfected). The iron (or steel) would be scored or undercut in a delicate pattern, and other metals in wire form, such as gold, silver, or copper, would be hammered in.

During the Middle Ages wooden doors and FURNITURE were frequently secured with iron hinges, straps, and locks; some were treated decoratively with profusions of scrolls, leaves, and flowers shaped by the blacksmith at the furnace while the iron was at white heat and then finished with punch and chisel. After about 1300 much wrought iron was worked cold at the bench, cut and sawn, filed and drilled in decorative patterns that could be assembled into railings, gates, and screens. Most blacksmiths and ironworkers were anonymous, but England's best smith, the French-born craftsman

Hasp, 1770–1800. Made in Lancaster County, Pennsylvania. Painted wrought iron, 15 x 8¾ in. (38.1 x 22.2 cm). Philadelphia Museum of Art; Titus C. Geesy Collection.

Jean Tijou, became famous for his book of designs for ironwork (published in London in 1693) and for the elaborate gates, railings, and screens he executed for WILLIAM AND MARY at Hampton Court Palace. Tijou combined traditional forge work with sheet iron, which he decorated in relief by hammering out the designs from the back in repoussé like a silversmith. When cast iron became more widely available in the eighteenth century, the hand methods and traditional techniques of the smith declined, although both cast and forged iron and steel were used to make and decorate luxury furniture in France and in Russia (at the Tula ironworks). Cast iron became the "new" material of the nineteenth century, used by architects as diverse as Karl Friedrich Schinkel in Berlin and Hector Guimard in Paris to decorate their cities with railings, bridges, candelabra, lampposts, and subway stops. It was also used to make jewelry and small household items, especially in Germany.

IVORY

Ivory—principally elephant tusk but also the tusks of walruses and fossil mammoths (found beneath melting Siberian snows) and the teeth of hippopotamuses, sperm whales, and other animals—is a whitish, hard, finely textured substance that has been much prized for carving, engraving, and decorative embellishment since the beginnings of civilization. Other substances have been used as substitutes for ivory—horn, antler, and bone (especially when polished), and more recently, plastics—although they cannot match its density or subtlety of color. The use of ivory in the West has been dependent on the vagaries of international trade, warfare, and economic expansion; today, strict regulations control the import and export of works that include even small amounts of ivory if it comes from endangered species.

The European trade in ivory was extensive during the Middle Ages, when it was used for RELIGIOUS OBJECTS (diptychs and triptychs, reliquaries, and bishops' croziers) and for secular ones (combs, mirror backs, caskets, and oliphants, or ceremonial and drinking urns). Ivory was widely available again during the seventeenth century as a result of the European journeys of exploration. BAROQUE marquetry FURNITURE often exploited the brilliant contrast of white ivory inlaid in figurative and naturalistic designs with ebony and other dark woods. Ivory was used for crucifixes and religious STATUETTES (notably in Italy and Germany), carved tankards and cups (frequently fitted with silver mounts), stocks and butts of guns, knife handles, spoons, snuffboxes, sword hilts, and game pieces. During the eighteenth and nineteenth centuries, ivory was carved with great decorative verve for many other small items as well (and brought in as EXPORT WARES from China)—toilet articles, toothpicks, tobacco rasps (for making snuff), FANS, jewelry, and billiard balls. The revival styles of the nineteenth century imitated the historical uses of ivory, and religious statuettes and copies of medieval relief carvings made in Dieppe in provincial France and in the major cities of Germany were prevalent during the GOTHIC REVIVAL. In the later nineteenth century, France and Belgium encouraged the use of ivory from their African colonies, making it available cheaply to artists, and it was used for small sculptures by Louis-Ernest Barrias and Moreau-Vauthier (Augustin-Jean Moreau) and in jewelry by René Lalique. During the ART DECO period, it was stylishly set off with painted bronze in statuettes by the Romanian sculptor Dcmêtre Chiparus and the German Ferdinand Preiss and inlaid in the furniture of Emile-Jacques Ruhlmann and Süe et Mare.

An isolated expression of FOLK ART in ivory is scrimshaw—designs of figures, ships, and animals engraved on whale teeth by whalers, as well as other small articles they made from ivory.

JACOBEAN

▷ **WHO** ARCHITECTS, ARTISTS, AND DESIGNERS: Inigo Jones, Sir Anthony Van Dyck
CRAFTSMEN AND MANUFACTURERS: William Benood, Francis Cleyn,
Sir Francis Crane, Sir Robert Mansell, William Maundy, John Plummer,
Christian van Vianen

▷ **WHEN** 1603 to 1649

▷ **WHERE** England

▷ **WHAT** The Jacobean period (it takes its name from Jacobus, Latin for James) includes the reigns of James I, the first Stuart king of England (reigned 1603–25), and his son Charles I (reigned 1625–49). During this age of increasing internationalism, foreign artists, among them Sir Anthony Van Dyck, came to work for the court and luxurious furnishings were imported from all over Europe and the Orient. The arrival of numerous foreign craftsmen helped English industry compete with the commerce in imported luxury goods. The manufacture of soda GLASS in the Venetian style, which had been initiated during the TUDOR period, developed further after a monopoly was granted to Sir Robert Mansell in 1623 to be the sole manufacturer of table glass, window glass, mirrors, and glass vessels. The tin-glazed POTTERY known as English "delftware" began to be made at factories in Lambeth, Southwark, and Bristol in the form of blue-and-white tableware and wine bottles

Press Cupboard, 1610. English. Oak, 63³/₄ x 59 x 15¹/₂ in.
(161.9 x 149.9 x 39.4 cm). Victoria and Albert Museum, London.

decorated with simple designs and inscriptions as well as large polychrome dishes decorated with figures. Finally, the weaving of TAPESTRIES was undertaken in London at the Mortlake workshop, founded by James I in 1619 in emulation of the Paris factory that Henri IV had built, also to supplant foreign imports. Using mostly Flemish weavers, Mortlake achieved a level of quality equal to that of the finest Continental tapestries. James's son, the future Charles I, commissioned the factory's first series, after paintings in the important collection he had formed, and he acquired Raphael's renowned tapestry cartoons for the Acts of the Apostles (now at the Victoria and Albert Museum, London) to serve as patterns for Mortlake weaving.

While many Tudor furniture forms continued to be made, new ones were introduced, such as triangular chairs turned completely on the lathe; gateleg tables; high-back settles; and so-called farthingale chairs fully upholstered (with velvets, silks, leather, and the coarse NEEDLEWORK imitating oriental CARPETS called "Turkey work") and studded with nails. In architecture, Inigo Jones introduced Italian forms, notably those of Andrea Palladio, in the Banqueting House at Whitehall Palace in London (1619–22) and the Queen's House in Greenwich (1616–35). The sobriety and symmetry of Jones's buildings contrasted with the Tudor style of picturesque country houses with bay windows, turrets, and gables and Flemish Mannerist ornamentation.

As the period progressed, this classical Italian bent favored by Charles I and the increasingly powerful Puritans signaled a new restraint throughout the decorative arts. The shapes and decoration of ornamental metalwork, for example, became simpler, and plain silver replaced silver gilt. Furniture too became less ostentatious, with bulbous legs and deep carving replaced by slender, turned supports and flattened ornamentation. Following the Jacobean period, during the Civil War and Oliver Cromwell's Commonwealth, activity in the decorative arts came to a virtual standstill.

JAPANISM—*see* AESTHETIC MOVEMENT

JAPANNING—*see* LACQUER

JUDAICA

Judaica embraces objects relating to all aspects of Jewish life: RELIGIOUS OBJECTS associated with public and private worship (Torah ornaments, prayer shawls), including those for the Sabbath (kiddush, or wine, cups; Sabbath

Spice Container, 17th–18th century. Made in Venice. Silver filigree, parcel gilt, and cloisonné enamels, height: 16½ in. (41.9 cm). The Jewish Museum, New York; Gift of Dr. Harry G. Friedman.

lamps) and other holidays (Hanukkah menorahs, Passover Seder plates); articles that mark the cycle of life of the observant Jew (mezuzahs, circumcision plates); and items relating to the Jewish community (alms boxes). In addition, it includes articles made by Jews (samplers with Hebrew lettering, GEORGIAN silver by Abraham de Oliveyra of London or Myer Myers of New York) and meaningful objects owned by them, which preserve the identity and enrich the history of the Jewish people.

The design of Jewish ritual objects reflects two forces: the conformity with religious rules and traditions—which vary according to whether they were made for Ashkenazic (eastern European) or Sephardic (originally Spanish) Jews—and the general design preferences, of both Jewish and Gentile craftsmen, that prevailed in the communities within which Jews lived. Thus, most ritual objects throughout the Diaspora retain the overall forms and symbols of prototypes dating back centuries, but the details of their decorative vocabulary are borrowed from a succession of European styles.

Specific types of objects can be associated with historically large centers of Jewish population: Italy, Germany, the Netherlands, England, Russia, and Poland. The single most impressive group comprises the BAROQUE silver-gilt Torah ornaments and ceremonial objects made for the court Jews of Germany by the master silversmiths of Augsburg, Nuremberg, and Frankfurt. Other notable metalwork includes Venetian silver filigree spice boxes in tower form from the seventeenth and eighteenth centuries and Polish ones decorated with birds, fish, fruit, and flowers during the eighteenth and nineteenth centuries. The communities of Bohemia and Moravia specialized in embroidering textiles for the synagogue, notably curtains and valences for the Holy Ark, using fine, sometimes antique, textiles. Italian and German communities embroidered Torah binders for presentation to the synagogue in commemoration of special occasions, such as circumcisions and marriages.

Since each Jewish household was expected to have its own array of ceremonial objects, they were once very plentiful, but the upheavals of persecution and emigration and the devastation during the Nazi period dispersed or destroyed much of this material. In the postwar era great efforts have been made to gather together the objects that have survived, many of which are now in museums, historical institutions, and large private collections.

JUGENDSTIL—*see* ART NOUVEAU

LACE

Lace, an openwork fabric of great delicacy, is the most intricate NEEDLEWORK craft. There are two distinct lace-making techniques. Needle lace, which first appeared in Italy during the sixteenth century, notably with the free-lace *punto in aria* (stitches in the air) technique, is made like embroidery—stitch by stitch with a single thread and a needle, following patterns on paper or parchment. Bobbin lace, of sixteenth-century Flemish and Italian origin, is made by twisting, plaiting, and knotting many threads wound on bobbins, or skeins, and held in place by pins that mark out the pattern on a pillow or bolster; hence its alternative name, *pillow lace.*

Beginning in the sixteenth century, lace was made in great quantities for ecclesiastical use (altar cloths, veils, and vestments), household linens and decoration, ceremonial costume, and fashionable clothing. Portraits show the popularity of lace over the centuries, from seventeenth-century Dutch burghers in dark garb set off with collars and sleeves of the finest Flemish bobbin lace, to George Washington with shirt ruffles of eighteenth-century French needle lace and Victorian women with lace falling from their hair in streamers, or lappets, wearing lace flounces, and holding lace-covered FANS.

A great deal of experience is required to differentiate the many types of lace and to apply the complicated lace nomenclature elaborated over the centuries. The names still most commonly used are based on French classification, derived from the centers that specialized in each type of lace, but now they generally refer to the techniques rather than the place of origin of any particular example. *Gros point de Venise,* a style of needle lace worked in large foliate patterns and over padding to produce effects of depth, originated in Venice and was favored throughout Europe until the end of the seventeenth century; Flemish needle lace offered competition because of the fineness of its threads. French styles, which developed with the factories established by Jean-Baptiste Colbert, minister of LOUIS XIV, then dominated needle lace, with smaller, flat designs and large areas of plain fill or mesh, called *point de France.* Eighteenth-century needle laces were classified according to their ground, with the most popular French needle laces being *point d'Alençon* and *point d'Argentan,* both with hexagonal fill. Bobbin laces were more easily and thus less expensively produced. Among the high-quality bobbin laces of the eighteenth century were the very fine Valenciennes floral lace, Mechlin lace, and *point d'Angleterre* lace (named for its popularity in England rather than its place of manufacture).

Section of a Needle-Made Reticella Band, early 17th century.
English or Spanish. Linen, length: 6 in. (15.2 cm). Cooper-Hewitt,
National Museum of Design, Smithsonian Institution, New York;
Bequest of Richard C. Greenleaf.

PILLOW, OR BOBBIN, TECHNIQUE

Handmade nineteenth-century laces, including the black lace fashionable at midcentury, were augmented by machine-made varieties. A type of coarse openwork fabric, mass produced for curtains and household decoration, became popular with large segments of the working population. The first machines, made in the late eighteenth century, could produce only simple mesh or net, to which decoration was added by hand or machine, but later their capabilities extended to making designs of the most splendid intricacy modeled after traditional types of lace, which could be distinguished from handmade examples only with the greatest difficulty. In the late nineteenth and early twentieth century, the making of lace by hand was revived by crafts schools and workshops, by museums, and in traditional lace-making centers such as Burano in Venice, where designs in ART NOUVEAU and modern styles were created along with those copied from historical examples and early pattern books.

LACQUER

True oriental lacquer—a hard, lustrous, durable colored finish for furniture and other objects achieved through the laborious application of many layers of the sap of an Eastern species of sumac *(Rhus verniciflua)*—was not commercially produced in the West before the early part of this century, when it appeared in France in the work of the ART DECO designers Eileen Gray and Jean Dunand. Rather, substitute processes (some almost as complicated) utilizing shellacs and varnishes were developed to imitate it, beginning in the seventeenth century, as craftsmen all over Europe tried to replicate the formulas that gave such brilliance to the cabinets, chests, and screens being imported in large numbers from the East. Today the term *lacquer* is generally applied to this work, but for several centuries these techniques were known as "japanning," or "japan work" (*japan* being adopted—like *china* for porcelain—as a generic reference to the technique's Asian origins). Many of the formulas used for this work were collected and published in England as early as 1688 in *A Treatise on Japanning and Varnishing* by John Stalker and George Parker.

The fashion for japan work was closely tied in the eighteenth century to the popularity of CHINOISERIE, and entire rooms were furnished with lacquer panels and decorations in the Chinese taste. Chairs, beds, tables, mirrors, musical instruments, clocks, trays, and other small articles in current European styles were also japanned—most frequently with raised, gilded chinoiserie decoration on black lacquer, but vermilion, blue, yellow, and green were also favored, particularly in England. In France in 1730 Guillaume and Etienne-Simon Martin patented a lacquerlike finish with a brilliant sheen and lighter and clearer colors, including light green, pale yellow, and pure white, which was widely imitated and came to be known as *vernis Martin*. They supplied ROCOCO lacquer decorations and furnishings for the apartments of Louis XV, Mme de Pompadour, and Frederick the Great, and both their plain and their decorated panels were incorporated into furniture by many of the finest cabinetmakers. *Vernis Martin* was also used for small objects and accessories, such as inkstands, pillboxes, and FANS.

Japanning was also used to decorate TIN ware (called "toleware" in the United States), in a lengthy process that required the firing of successive coats of varnish, which was first developed in Pontypool in Wales in the early eighteenth century. Braziers, candlesticks, tea and coffee urns, and trays with a heat-resistant finish were produced in great numbers by the Pontypool factory, which was run for a century and a half by the family of Thomas Allgood. In nineteenth-century England, Birmingham became the center of japanning, with Jennens & Bettridge using this technique to decorate a large line of tea trays and other small items made of PAPIER-MÂCHÉ.

Among the noted centers of European lacquer production were Spa in Belgium, where walking sticks, toilet sets, and small pieces of furniture were made in large quantities during the seventeenth and eighteenth centuries; Berlin, where a craftsman from Spa, Gérard Dagly, produced lacquered furniture and musical instruments under a monopoly granted in 1696 by the elector of Brandenburg, Frederick II; and Danilkovo in Russia, where from 1824 Piotr Lukutin created his famed snuffboxes, many painted with Russian scenes.

LIGHTING

The forms of lighting devices and lamps vary according to the source of fuel (wood, oil, candle, gas, kerosene, or electricity), the vessels used to contain and control the fuel source, and the reflectors employed to diffuse or concentrate the light. Wood and rush (stripped and soaked in fat) have been the most basic fuels, used since antiquity; wood was burned in torches, iron cressets or baskets, and splint holders, and rush in metal holders (rushlights). Longer burning and more easily portable than wood or rush, vegetable and fish oils and grease were also used, burned in shallow pans of metal (usually bronze or iron) or terra-cotta vessels, with reed, rag, or twisted flax for a wick. Immersed or enclosed at one end, the wick absorbed and drew up the oil, supplying fuel to the flame that burned at the free end. Small oil lamps, with a handle at one end and a spout for the flame at the other, were made virtually everywhere, but they did not give an especially good light; they constantly had to be filled and the wick had to be trimmed.

Antique models were the source for the bronze oil lamps made in the shapes of figures and mythological creatures by the Paduan sculptor Andrea Riccio during the RENAISSANCE. In the sixteenth century, oil lamps were also made with a bottle-shaped reservoir above the spout, which helped regulate the flow of air to the flame, but it was not until the late eighteenth century that radical improvements were made to the oil lamp—notably by Aimé Argand, a Swiss chemist who invented a new type of tube-shaped wick. With a font or reservoir for the oil at one side and a glass chimney above, he set the wick between two metal cylinders within an upright metal tube, which brought oxygen to the flame from both the interior and the exterior and caused it to burn more brightly and with less smoke. Argand-type lamps were made in the nineteenth century by the firms of Boulton in England, Quinquet in France, and Cornelius in America, in both table and hanging models. Reliable and relatively clean, such oil lamps provided stronger illumination, but they still required frequent filling. They were made in functional shapes, with the reservoir, glass chimney, and vertical wick often left undisguised. From the 1860s, kerosene (a newly discovered petroleum product) replaced traditional fuel oils because it produced a better flame.

Candles, made of flax threads coated with pitch and wax or both, were known in antiquity, but it was not until the Middle Ages that tallow and beeswax candles as we know them today were made. By the fifteenth century they were molded as well as hand dipped, and in the mid-nineteenth century they began to be molded by machine. The earliest type of candle-holder or candlestick was a pricket, usually made of metal (but also of ceramic), with a metal spike to hold the candle and a drip pan at its base to catch the wax. From about the fifteenth century, domestic candlesticks were usually fitted with a socket to hold a single candle or with arms and nozzles for more than one candle—a construction known as a *candelabrum.* Candles were also burned in lanterns; in wall brackets, or sconces, fitted from the seventeenth century with polished brass, silver, or mirrored backplates to reflect the light; and in brass or glass chandeliers suspended from the ceiling, the latter furnished with drops and chains of glass that caught the light. In the seventeenth century, candlesticks with one or more holders

BALDWIN GARDINER (1827–1845).
"Argand" Oil Lamp, 1835(?)–40. American. Gilt bronze and glass,
height: 17³/₄ in. (45 cm). The Metropolitan Museum of Art, New York;
Gift of John C. Cattus.

were often placed on candlestands, a new form of furniture made in several sizes, sometimes together with a pier table and mirror in which the lights would be reflected.

In the late eighteenth and early nineteenth centuries, the newly discovered gas fuel was applied to lighting, although it was not until the mid-nineteenth century that gas lamps came into widespread use, with the development of a burner with a top made of steatite (a stone that did not corrode and that prevented heat from escaping) and with the invention of a gas mantle that became incandescent when heated, which produced a safe lamp and a brilliant white light. Clean, easy to use, and smokeless, gas lamps soon largely replaced oil lamps. First used in factories and for streetlights, they were quickly adapted to domestic use as municipal gasworks made fuel available to well-to-do homes in most major Western cities. They were made primarily in the form of wall lamps and chandeliers (known as "gasoliers" in the United States), which starting in the 1830s could be lowered or raised.

The history of lighting was revolutionized when Thomas Edison invented the electric lightbulb in 1879, using a carbon (later tungsten) filament enclosed in a glass container and brought to white heat by an electric current. Edison's small lightbulb replaced all the bulky apparatus required by combustion lighting; it was much more efficient and could fit anywhere into a socket, like a candle in a candlestick. No longer dependent on a vertical flame, the new light source could be positioned in a variety of ways. At the turn of the century, ART NOUVEAU designers like Richard Riemerschmid sometimes left the bulbs exposed, suspended from the ceiling on the electric wires, as modernist designers were also to do in the 1920s. For the most part, however, Art Nouveau electric fixtures, made largely of metal (usually bronze) were designed in naturalistic, particularly floral shapes, with bulbs blossoming above plant stems that concealed the wires.

LOUIS XIII—*see* BAROQUE, LOUIS XIV

LOUIS XIV

▷ **WHO** ARCHITECTS, ARTISTS, AND DESIGNERS: Jean Berain, Paul Androuet Du Cerceau, Charles Le Brun, Jean Lepautre
CRAFTSMEN AND MANUFACTURERS: Claude I Ballin, Claude II Ballin, André-Charles Boulle, Domenico Cucci, Nicolas Delaunay, Gobelins tapestry factory, Pierre Gole, Alexandre-Jean Oppenordt, Savonnerie carpet factory

▷ **WHEN** 1643 to 1715

▷ **WHERE** France

▷ **WHAT** The BAROQUE style that flourished in France during the reign of Louis XIV (1643–1715) reflected the personal, autocratic tastes of the monarch and the efficiency of his ministers Jules Cardinal Mazarin and Jean-Baptiste Colbert. They were responsible for furnishing and decorating the royal residences and for dispensing the vast sums of money that made these residences symbols of the king's wealth and power. In the process, they patronized native industries—tapestry, glass, and furniture among them—making France a leader in European fashion and providing some degree of economic self-sufficiency in luxury products.

In 1662 Colbert founded the Manufacture Royale des Meubles de la Couronne (Royal Manufactory of Crown Furnishings) to supply the needs of the court and royal palaces as well as gifts required by the king. It employed both French and foreign craftsmen (particularly those from Italy and Holland), including the cabinetmakers Domenico Cucci and Pierre Gole, and provided workshops for the weaving of high- and low-warp TAPESTRIES, embroidery and painting on silk, silverwork, wood carving, gilding of wood and metal, work in bronze, mosaic work in hardstones, and cabinetmaking. The factory was directed by the painter Charles Le Brun, who supplied most of the designs, ensuring a centralized system for the development of the decorative arts and a unified style based on Le Brun's preference for Italian Baroque forms These were distinguished by their grand scale, precious materials, and classical motifs treated in a heavy, sculptural manner. Le Brun's interiors at Versailles—with their deep-toned mythological and allegorical paintings inserted in geometrical compartments in walls and ceilings, elaborately molded stucco ornament, colored marble paneling, carved and painted or gilded woodwork, and marquetry floors—recalled Italian palace decoration. New and conspicuously extravagant was Le Brun's use of mirrored glass on walls, notably in the Grande Galerie at Versailles (1679–86), and silver furnishings (massive solid-silver tables detailed with figures and vases on stands by Claude I Ballin), which he installed there and in the king's bedroom. All the Versailles silver furniture and household plate were melted down in 1689 to pay the king's war costs—a process repeated in 1709.

The dazzling luxury that Louis XIV demanded affected all of the craft trades. The richest furnishing materials, including raised embroideries on a background of silk brocade with elaborate fringes, were supplied to Versailles. Cucci produced the grandest of furniture, including ornamental cabinets veneered in ebony and decorated with gilt-bronze and hardstone mosaics of jasper, agate, and lapis. André-Charles Boulle developed complex marquetries (see FURNITURE) in arabesque patterns after designs by Jean Berain, made of decorative woods, tortoiseshell, and brass, and he popularized them in a new furniture form—the commode, or chest of drawers.

The dignity and ceremony of the court were reflected in such formal devices as symmetry, balance, and the use of centralized motifs. Particularly significant were motifs that included the insignia of the monarchy—two interlaced *L*s (Louis XIV's cipher), the fleur-de-lis, and the sunburst (emblem of the Sun King)—and those derived from classical antiquity (masks, shells, trophies or decorations of arms, terms, caryatids, and pilasters). The most spectacular use of such motifs was in the ninety-three Savonnerie CARPETS woven for the Grande Galerie of the Louvre (1668–89), conceived as a unified scheme glorifying the king; each was decorated with framed panels and symbolic devices and surrounded by acanthus scrolls on a black ground and gadrooned borders. By the end of his reign, however, the king had grown tired of such vast schemes and of the pomp and insistent grandeur with which he was surrounded, requesting from his architects and decorators the lighter, simpler interiors and furnishings that ushered in the RÉGENCE style.

LOUIS XV

▷ **WHO** ARCHITECTS, ARTISTS, AND DESIGNERS: Lambert-Sigisbert Adam, Jacques-François Blondel, Germain Boffrand, François Boucher, Ange-Jacques Gabriel, Christophe Huet, Philippe de Lasalle, Juste-Aurèle Meissonnier, Gilles-Marie Oppenord, Nicolas Pineau, Jean Revel, Paul-Ambroise Slodtz, Sébastien-Antoine Slodtz, Antoine Watteau CRAFTSMEN AND MANUFACTURERS: Beauvais tapestry factory, Chantilly porcelain factory, Nicolas-Quinibert Foliot, Antoine-Robert Gaudreaux, François-Thomas Germain, Thomas Germain, Gobelins tapestry factory, Gilles Joubert, Mennecy porcelain factory, Jacques Roettiers, Saint-Cloud porcelain factory, Savonnerie carpet factory, Sèvres porcelain factory, Strasbourg pottery factory, Jean-Baptiste I Tilliard, Jean-Baptiste II Tilliard, Bernard II Van Risen Burgh

▷ **WHEN** 1715 to 1774

▷ **WHERE** France

After **CHARLES-ANTOINE COYPEL** (1694–1752).
Tapestry: Don Quixote Guided by Folly, 1780–83. Woven by the
Gobelins manufactory, Paris. Wool and silk, 12 ft. 2 in. x 11 ft. 8 in. (4.22
x 3.56 m). Philadelphia Museum of Art; Gift of Mrs. Widener Dixon.

▷ **WHAT** The reign of Louis XV in France (1715–74), which included the regency of Philippe, duc d'Orléans (see RÉGENCE), is identified with the ROCOCO style, although NEOCLASSICISM had already come into fashion at the time of the king's death. Unlike LOUIS XIV, who lived formally at Versailles in public rooms of state, Louis XV created a private life there in smaller apartments *(petits appartements)* whose intimate spaces imposed a reduced scale of architectural ornament. The taste for nature and intimacy was evident in new subjects developed by artists and designers, including Antoine Watteau's *fêtes galantes* (courtship idylls played outdoors by gallant shepherds and shepherdesses, hunters and huntresses, satyrs and nymphs) and Christophe Huet's and François Boucher's satirical and exotic variants peopled with monkeys *(singeries)* and Chinese figures (see CHINOISERIE). The Louis XV style pervaded the fine and decorative arts, from garden sculptures by Lambert-Sigisbert Adam, which included ornamental figures for the cascade at Saint-Cloud and the Neptune fountain at Versailles, to book design. Publishers abandoned the large formats favored in the seventeenth century for smaller volumes decorated with intricately engraved title pages and printers' flowers, ornaments, and decorated initials. Just as texts often became secondary to the decorated page, so TAPESTRIES were designed as framed pictures, a pretext for elaborate surrounding decorations of flower garlands, cartouches, trophies, and animals, as in the Don Quixote series by Charles-Antoine Coypel woven at Gobelins. The previously favored vast classical compositions on carpets were supplanted at the Savonnerie factory by designs that combined flowers, garlands, and bouquets with scrolling arabesques and bat wings. At the same time, Jean Revel introduced a new painterly naturalism to the design of silks by shading flowers as if they were three-dimensional.

The reign of Louis XV saw the rise of PORCELAIN manufacture in France at the factories of Saint-Cloud, Chantilly, Mennecy, and Sèvres, the last-named taken over and protected in 1759 by the king, who became its chief client. The soft-paste porcelain produced by these factories, with its glassy, soft white surface, provided a lustrous background for painted decorations. At Sèvres, ornamental painting was most fully exploited, and colored enameled grounds and ornamental gilding, which only Sèvres was privileged to use, were also developed. Naturalistic subjects with flowers, birds, and figures predominated among the painted decorations on porcelain as well as on POTTERY; at the Strasbourg pottery factory, tureens made in the form of vegetables and animals were colored realistically. The same naturalism appeared in silverwares, including table services with cast centerpieces and tureens featuring hunt motifs of dogs, rabbits, birds, and dead game made for the court by Thomas Germain and Jacques Roettiers. Furniture in sinuous shapes reflected the increasing taste for informal living and comfort, with such new seat forms as the small semicircular armchair *(fauteuil de bureau)*, upholstered daybed composed of separate parts *(duchesse-brisée)*, and sofa with closed ends *(sultane)*. Elaborate and colorful decorations often appeared to dissolve the structure of case furniture. Floral marquetry (see FURNITURE); swirling gilt-bronze mounts; polychrome LACQUER; carved scrolls, flowers, and shells; and even porcelain plaques decorated with flowers enlivened the Louis XV vocabulary of Rococo furniture ornament. The use of such varied materials for furniture reached its height during the period of LOUIS XVI.

LOUIS XVI

▷ **WHO** ARCHITECTS AND DESIGNERS: François-Joseph Bélanger, Juste-François Boucher, Jean-Charles Delafosse, Jean-Démosthène Dugourc, Jean-François de Neufforge
CRAFTSMEN AND MANUFACTURERS: Robert-Joseph Auguste, Martin Carlin, Jacques Gondouin, Pierre Gouthière, Georges Jacob, Jean-Henri Riesener, Jacques-Nicolas Roettiers, Sèvres porcelain factory, Adam Weisweiler

▷ **WHEN** 1774 to 1793

▷ **WHERE** France

▷ **WHAT** When Louis XVI became king in 1774, NEOCLASSICISM was already flourishing in France. ROCOCO had all but disappeared, and furniture and interiors were classical in inspiration. Rooms decorated with fluted pilasters or columns and with coffered ceilings housed furniture with tapering and fluted legs, richly decorated with marquetry (see FURNITURE), carving, gilding, and finely wrought gilt-bronze mounts of classical design, including caryatid and sphinx forms. Chairs with straight legs and oval, square, or trapezoidal backs were carved with ornaments derived from classical architecture, such as scrolls, frets, and husks. The most original aspect of Louis XVI furniture was its use of decorative (usually floral) plaques of Sèvres PORCELAIN, a fashion developed by the art dealer Simon-Philippe Poirier and his successor Dominique Daguerre, who hired Martin Carlin, Adam Weisweiler, and others to execute porcelain-mounted furniture. In the 1780s a reaction set in against such lavish expenditures, and a more austere style of Neoclassicism developed, characterized in furniture by the use of simple veneers of plain woods. Metalwork forms were also simplified and given spare decorations associated with classical architecture, including acanthus leaves, fluting, and gadrooning. This severe form of Neoclassicism persisted after the French Revolution during the Directoire (1795–99), for economic as well as aesthetic reasons.

LOUIS-PHILIPPE

▷ **WHO** ARCHITECTS, ARTISTS, AND DESIGNERS: Claude-Aimé Chenavard; Jean-Jacques Feuchère; Léon Feuchère; Jean-Baptiste-Jules Klagmann; Henri-Joseph-François, baron de Triqueti
CRAFTSMEN AND MANUFACTURERS: Eck et Durand, François-Désiré Froment-Meurice, Guillaume Grohé, Georges-Alphonse Jacob-Desmalter, Jean Lapeyre, Georges-Alphonse-Bonifacio Monbro, Sèvres porcelain factory, Antoine Vechte

▷ **WHEN** 1830 to 1848

▷ **WHERE** France

▷ **WHAT** *Louis-Philippe* is a useful, if imprecise, label for the richly varied revival styles that flourished in France during the reign of the Orléans king Louis-Philippe (1830–48) and culminated in the SECOND EMPIRE. Louis-Philippe advanced the taste for historicism that spread in the mid-nineteenth century from France and England throughout Europe and to America. Committed to restoring the royal palaces of Saint-Cloud, Fontainebleau, Compiègne, Versailles, and others, the king insisted that these buildings be refurnished according to their original styles, whether Gothic, RENAISSANCE, LOUIS XIV, LOUIS XV, or LOUIS XVI. The revival of these styles in France therefore contained a strong element of nationalism.

The ornamentalist Claude-Aimé Chenavard, who during the 1830s provided designs for the royal porcelain factory at Sèvres and published designs for furniture and textiles as well as ceramics, was instrumental in popularizing the Renaissance style. The sculptural vocabulary of grotesques, foliage, and mythological figures that he introduced appeared in works shown in the national trade exhibitions held in Paris in 1834, 1839, and 1844, as well as in palace furnishings characterized by massive forms and deeply carved ornament. In the later years of Louis-Philippe's reign, the RENAISSANCE REVIVAL style found itself in competition with a revival of the Louis XV (see ROCOCO REVIVAL) and Louis XVI styles, although these acquired in this context a solidity, heaviness, and tendency toward the florid, which they had lacked in the eighteenth century. The taste for mid-eighteenth-century fashions was led by the

Vase, 1834–35. Made by the Sèvres porcelain factory. Hard-paste porcelain, with gilt-bronze mounts, height: 36 in. (91.5 cm). Musée National de Céramique, Sèvres, France.

king from about 1840: he ordered modern Louis XV chairs and case pieces with curved (cabriole) legs and gilded surfaces, as well as a suite of tapestried furniture in the Louis XVI style for his daughter the princess Clémentine.

MANNERISM—*see* RENAISSANCE

MARKS, SIGNATURES, AND LABELS

Attributing an antique to a specific designer, craftsperson, or manufacturer and dating it precisely can add greatly to its value and significance. Attribution is best achieved when the piece bears a mark, signature, or label, although this is not a guarantee of authenticity because such elements are not always authentic or original to a piece. Furniture stamps and woven tapestry factory marks, for example, can be added after the fact, or "let in," although signs of such alterations are usually evident.

As indications of authorship and product identification, signatures can be obvious elements (names painted on the dials of clocks or woven into the corners of American jacquard coverlets); others can be discreet and may have to be discovered. Labels, usually made of paper and printed, are generally applied out of view.

Signatures and labels appear in many different forms, but marks—notably those on FURNITURE, GOLD AND SILVER, PEWTER, PORCELAIN, POTTERY, and TAPESTRIES —belong to standardized (sometimes official) systems of identification. These can provide significant information about the origins of objects. Starting in the Middle Ages, many tapestries were marked with factory identifications and signatures; in the sixteenth century, in order to maintain quality production and protect the reputation of the major tapestry centers, the use of marks became legally regulated. For example, one law, established in the Low Countries in 1544, required tapestries to bear the marks of the weaver or manufacturer and of the town in which they were made.

Furniture makers have sometimes stamped or labeled their work. Among the best known are the Parisian makers of the eighteenth century, who were obliged by the 1743–51 statutes of their guild, the Corporation des Menuisiers-Ebénistes, to mark their furniture with their names before it could be sold, using an iron stamp *(maindron)*. The guild authorities also inspected their furniture to ensure that it met the required standards of quality. When the furniture was approved for sale, it was stamped with the

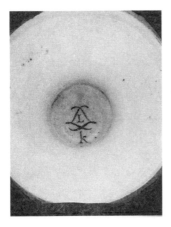

Marks on the underside of a French porcelain vase, Philadelphia Museum of Art. The interlacing *L*s stand for the Sèvres royal porcelain factory, the single Roman *L* represents the year 1764, and the *k* identifies Charles-Nicolas Dodin as its decorative painter.

Stamps beneath the front rail of a writing table, Philadelphia Museum of Art.
M Carlin is the stamp of the master cabinetmaker Martin Carlin, and *JME* is the monogram of the guild of furniture makers (Jurande des Menuisiers-Ebénistes).

Marks on the underside of an English silver plate, Philadelphia Museum of Art. *WF* is the mark of the maker, William Fountain; the lion passant is the standard, or sterling, mark; the leopard's head crowned is the mark of the London assay office; the *C* is the date letter for 1798–99; and the sovereign's head is the duty mark indicating that a duty of sixpence per ounce had been paid by the silversmith at the time of the assay.

monogram JME (for Jurande [wardenship] des Menuisiers-Ebénistes). Craftsmen employed by the crown were exempt from these regulations.

Assay marks (or hallmarks) have been stamped on almost all works in gold and silver made in Europe (but not officially in the United States) from late in the Middle Ages to today. Official guarantees of the standard of the metal's purity, they have regulated value and assured that the appropriate taxes have been paid. Through symbols, initials, letters, and numerals, hallmarks indicate the city or country of origin of an object (a fleur-de-lis, for example, signifies France) and often its date (usually noted by a letter), designer, and maker. Silver and gold marks were registered with each municipality and can be traced today through facsimile illustrations in a number of standard dictionaries and compendiums, which decode their meanings. The pewter trade had a similar but less well-regulated system of hallmarks.

Ceramic marks (impressed or incised in the clay, painted under or over the glaze, or sometimes applied in relief) were used by factories to identify their products in the marketplace; additional marks designating designers, modelers, decorators, and other information about a piece were usually added for internal, not public, purposes. Factory marks and signatures had been used on ceramics in Italy and Holland in the sixteenth and seventeenth centuries, but ceramic marks came into regular use in Europe only after the Meissen factory introduced Europe's first hard-paste porcelain and its crossed-swords device in 1724 to assure authenticity and protect a growing foreign trade. The lack of regulations allowed competitors, especially foreign factories, to take advantage of the success of popular firms by imitating their marks. The mark of Meissen was imitated, for example, by eighteenth-century potteries in France (La Courtille) and Germany (Limbach) with symbols resembling Meissen's crossed swords; it was also openly copied by several eighteenth-century English factories, including Derby and Worcester. Ceramics marks for some individual factories are well documented, but many of the secondary marks are still unidentified—for example, those that indicate workmen (throwers, painters, gilders, assemblers), model numbers, and incised kiln notations.

MARQUETRY—*see* FURNITURE

MODERNISM

▷ **WHO** ARCHITECTS, ARTISTS, AND DESIGNERS: Aino Marsio Aalto, Alvar Aalto, Josef Albers, Erik Gunnar Asplund, Peter Behrens, Marcel Breuer, Pierre Chareau, Serge Chermayeff, Wells Coates, Theo van Doesburg, Eileen Gray, Hermann Gretsch, Walter Gropius, Poul Henningsen, René Herbst, Pierre Jeanneret, Francis Jourdain, Kaare Klint, Le Corbusier (Charles-Edouard Jeanneret), Kazimir Malevich, Robert Mallet-Stevens, Ludwig Mies van der Rohe, László Moholy-Nagy, Piet Mondrian, J. J. P. Oud, Charlotte Perriand, Lilly Reich, Gerrit Rietveld, Aleksandr Rodchenko, Adolf G. Schneck, Mart Stam, Bruno Taut, Giuseppe Terragni, Wilhelm Wagenfeld
CRAFTSMEN AND MANUFACTURERS: Anni Albers, Theodor Bogler, Marianne Brandt, Willem Hendrik Gispen, Wilhelm Kåge, Trude Petri, Gunta Stölzl, Thonet

▷ **WHEN** 1920s through 1930s

▷ **WHERE** Europe

▷ **WHAT** Although *modernism* has been used loosely to designate much of the design of this century, the term more accurately describes only one aspect of it—the progressive, or functionalist, design that emerged in Europe early in this period. Rejecting the norms of traditional, handcrafted decorative arts, the modernist aesthetic required design to indicate its machine origin through unornamented simplicity and economy; each object must be fit for its purpose, expressive of its structure, and "honest" in its use of materials.

The earliest designs made according to these principles appeared in Germany, most notably in the teakettles and lamps by Peter Behrens for the large electric company Allgemeine Elektricitäts-Gesellschaft (AEG) between 1907 and 1914. Abjuring ornamentation for utility and using standardized components for manufacturing efficiency, he introduced a smooth, geometric style, which he considered particularly appropriate for machine production. Two other architects, both associated with Behrens at one time, expanded modernism in the 1920s: Walter Gropius, who established the influential Bauhaus design school in Weimar, Germany, in 1919; and Le Corbusier, whose writings championed standardized utilitarian objects (what he called "equipment") over the decorative arts and whose statement that a house is a "machine for living in" became a principal tenet of International Style architecture and modernist design.

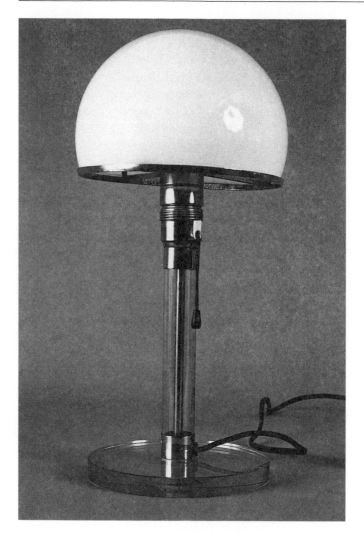

KARL J. JUCKER (active 1920–25)
and **WILHELM WAGENFELD** (1900–1990).
Table Lamp, 1923–24. German. Clear and opalescent glass,
nickel-plated brass, and steel, height: 15⅜ in. (38 cm).
Bauhaus-Archiv, Berlin.

Modernism is typified by the metal furniture invented by Marcel Breuer in 1925 and other of his designs in tubular steel made soon after—generally upholstered in leather, cane, or a strong canvaslike fabric known as "iron cloth" *(Eisengarn)*—which spread worldwide in the later 1920s and 1930s. Among the well-known work created in this medium were Mart Stam's and Ludwig Mies van der Rohe's cantilevered chairs of 1927 and the chaise longue designed by Le Corbusier in association with Charlotte Perriand and Pierre Jeanneret in 1929, all distributed internationally by Thonet. Although the modernist ideal was mass production, not all such design could be accommodated by large-scale manufacture, and designers often found themselves imitating with meticulous handwork the qualities of precision that signified the machine style. This was true of Mies van der Rohe's famous Barcelona chair and much of the early work of the Bauhaus, such as the metalwork and lighting of Marianne Brandt and Wilhelm Wagenfeld.

MOSAICS

The mosaic technique of arranging small pieces (tesserae) of glass, HARD-STONES, or ceramic into geometric or pictorial compositions has been practiced largely in Italy. In antiquity and the early Middle Ages, glass mosaics were widely used for architectural decoration, notably in the churches of Ravenna during the sixth century; the technique was revived in the late sixteenth century in Rome, especially by the Vatican Mosaic Workshop (Studio del Musaico della Reverenda Fabbrica di San Pietro), which was established to replace deteriorating paintings in Saint Peter's Basilica with mosaics and later undertook restoration of historical mosaics in churches elsewhere. In the late eighteenth century the Vatican workshop began a commercial operation to rival the work of independent mosaicists in Rome; their production has included micromosaics made with tiny pieces of glass, which were incorporated into furniture, boxes, plaques, and jewelry for export and the tourist trade.

NAPOLEON III—*see* SECOND EMPIRE

NEEDLEWORK

Needlework includes both embroidery, in which stitches create the decoration, and appliqué, in which fabrics are pieced, overlaid, and applied to a base fabric to form composite designs; other needlework techniques use needle and thread to produce whole fabrics, such as knitting, crocheting, and lace making. The embroiderer—using threads or yarns of silk, cotton, wool, and manmade fibers (and sometimes metallic strands, beads, sequins, and the like)—decorates fabrics using a variety of stitches. These range from the common in-and-out running stitch, X-shape cross-stitch, and satin stitch (used as fill) to the more complex Florentine, or flame, stitch for bargello work and the oblique Gobelins stitch, which gives the effect of tapestry weave. Depth can be added with padding, couching (stitching over other stitches), and stumpwork (a technique popular during the RESTORATION, in which embroidery details are raised and heavily padded, sometimes being made separately and applied to the fabric).

Embroidery was widely in evidence during the Middle Ages and the RENAISSANCE, when members of embroiderers guilds from Spain to Iceland would ornament ecclesiastical vestments and altar frontals with religious motifs and scenes in silk and metallic threads. Well-known fifteenth- and sixteenth-century Italian painters, such as Antonio Pollaiuolo and Perino del Vaga, created the cartoons (full-scale drawings) for such ecclesiastical embroideries. Cutwork (punto tagliato), in which the fabric is cut away, and drawnwork (punto tirato), in which threads are removed from the fabric, with the open areas then filled with embroidery, were also used for ecclesiastical articles in Italy, particularly Venice; these techniques ultimately led to the development of LACE.

Much domestic embroidery was produced in sixteenth- and seventeenth-century England. Elizabethan blackwork (done in black silk on a white ground) and JACOBEAN and Restoration crewel (woolen) figured embroidery in monochrome or multiple colors were used to adorn clothing, bed hangings, and UPHOLSTERY. Turkey work (needlework in plush stitch—that is, cut to produce a pile, in imitation of oriental carpets) was used for cushions as well as bed and table coverings, and quilting was used for whole-cloth bedcovers, clothing (notably petticoats), and piecework coverlets. Designs were based on manuscript illuminations, Indian palampores and other imported fabrics, and a number of popular pattern books, such as Richard Shorleyker's Schole-House for the Needle (1624). Such books were also a source of designs for the embroidered pictures and samplers, test pieces, and school pieces that were made throughout Europe and the Americas from the seventeenth·century. These demonstrate skill in such embroidery techniques as white work (white yarn on white cloth, often incorporating cutwork and drawnwork), darning, and stumpwork; their motifs include the alphabet, numbers, moralizing and biblical sayings, maps, and naturalistic scenes and elements.

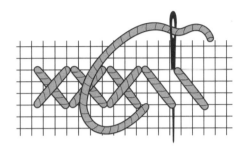

CROSS-STITCH

SATIN STITCH

PLUSH, OR TURKEY WORK, STITCH

The nineteenth century saw a craze for Berlin woolwork, made by copying hand-colored patterns on squared paper, which were originally issued by German publishers in the first decade of the century. Using these easy-to-follow patterns for a broad range of popular subjects, from animals and flowers to medieval and biblical scenes, amateur embroiderers worked designs in wool on canvas in simple cross and tent stitches. Later in the century the art needlework movement signaled both a return to earlier sources and techniques and the creation of modern designs for embroidery, including those by Lewis F. Day and William Morris. Elizabeth Wardle's Leek Embroidery Society and School of Embroidery (founded in 1879 in Leek, England) demonstrated the seriousness of its intent in 1885–86 by copying the famous eleventh-century Bayeux Tapestry (Ancien Evêché, Bayeux, France), a 231-foot-long (71 meters) woolen embroidery depicting the Norman conquest of England. ART NOUVEAU designers also created models for needlework, including whiplash designs by the German Hermann Obrist.

Appliqué is now most closely connected with the making of bedcovers, often quilted ones, using techniques that were transplanted by settlers from Europe to America during the eighteenth century. Certain patterns can be connected to particular regions and communities, but many of the designs were also transmitted across the continent as the country expanded; New England missionaries, for example, took quilt making to Hawaii as early as 1820. In one form of appliqué coverlet, which originated in England and was popular in America from the mid-eighteenth century, birds, flowers, and other naturalistic motifs were cut from English and French block-printed fabrics, then sewn to a ground fabric to form large scenes, often resembling Indian *palampores.* Appliqué quilts with smaller cut pictorial designs and repeated patterns required coordinated printed fabrics (usually bought new rather than salvaged) for the floral baskets, wreaths, and other motifs that were made into bride's quilts, friendship quilts, and album quilts (the last was a distinctive tradition in Baltimore). The pieced (or patchwork) technique, most popular from the mid-nineteenth century on, used designs made of solid-color fabrics or small prints cut from templates in decorative shapes such as snowflakes, tulips, leaves, and feathers, or of regular shapes that created abstract repeats with descriptive or evocative names such as sunburst, log cabin, courthouse steps, and prairie star. In the late nineteenth century, silk, velvet, and ribbon scraps embroidered with large feather and herringbone stitches were made into asymmetrical arrangements known as "crazy quilts," which show the influence of the arts of Japan (see AESTHETIC MOVEMENT).

NEOCLASSICISM

▷ **WHO** ARCHITECTS, ARTISTS, AND DESIGNERS: Nicolai Abraham Abildgaard, Robert Adam, François-Joseph Bélanger, Antonio Canova, William Chambers, Charles-Louis Clérisseau, Jacques-Louis David, Jean-Charles Delafosse, John Flaxman, George Hepplewhite, Jean-Baptiste Huet, Thomas Jefferson, Benjamin Henry Latrobe, Jean-François de Neufforge, Giovanni Battista Piranesi, Johann Gottfried Schadow, Karl Friedrich Schinkel, Thomas Sheraton, James "Athenian" Stuart
CRAFTSMEN AND MANUFACTURERS: Guillaume Benneman, Matthew Boulton, Georges Jacob, Giuseppe Maggiolini, Jean-François Oeben, Jean-Henri Riesener, David Roentgen, Giuseppe Valadier, Luigi Valadier, Josiah Wedgwood
THEORIST: Johann Joachim Winckelmann

▷ **WHEN** 1750s through 1840s

▷ **WHERE** Europe and America

▷ **WHAT** Neoclassicism—the revival of the architectural forms and ornamental motifs of classical antiquity (primarily Greek and Roman but also Etruscan and Egyptian)—emerged in Europe during the third quarter of the eighteenth century, spurred by the discoveries made at such archaeological sites as Herculaneum and Pompeii in Italy. Ancient ruins were studied systematically and published widely (notably by James "Athenian" Stuart and Nicholas Revett in *The Antiquities of Athens,* 1762). Eighteenth-century artists and designers were divided in their use of these archaeological sources. The sculptor Antonio Canova, and others who followed the theories of Johann Joachim Winckelmann (*Gedanken über die Nachahmung der griechischen Werke [Reflections on the Imitation of Greek Art],* 1755), were inspired by Greek art, particularly sculpture. They produced simple, solid, clear-cut, three-dimensional forms in a cool, austere manner that emphasized form and outline. Those like Robert ADAM, who followed Giovanni Battista Piranesi (*Della magnificenza ed architettura de' Romani [On the Magnificence and Architecture of the Romans],* 1761), found inspiration in Roman and Etruscan art, particularly the richly decorated style of the early Roman empire. Their work was complex and decorative, emphasizing surface and color. Most artists identified their aesthetics with ethics, claiming truth, nobility, and honesty for Neoclassicism on ancient authority, whether Greek or Roman. It was this concern for ethics that separated Neoclassicism from the prevailing ROCOCO style, which was criticized at the time for its immorality, irrationality, frivolity, and deception. Nevertheless, the continuing influence of the Rococo style can be seen in the light and elegant effect of certain Neoclassical works, such as Adam's "Etruscan" decorations.

Elements from varied sources of ancient architecture, sculpture, and furniture were borrowed, combined, and adapted to contemporary uses in an eclectic Neoclassical synthesis. The foliate scroll of a chair's armrest might mimic the volute of an Ionic capital, while the flutes of the seat rail might imitate a temple frieze. Winged mythological beasts such as the sphinx and griffin, carved in wood and gilded (or later cast in metal), were used to decorate furniture loosely following the precedent of Hellenistic Greek or Roman marble thrones and tables. A vocabulary of ancient ornament was assembled and applied everywhere by designers as diverse as Josiah Wedgwood in England and Nicolai Abraham Abildgaard in Denmark. It included acanthus (a plant with indented and scrolled leaves), anthemion (a stylized motif derived from the honeysuckle blossom or seed husk), egg and dart (a design of ovals alternating with dart or arrow forms), Greek key or fret (an angular meander pattern resembling interlocking rectangles), palmette (a symmetrical leaf or blossomlike motif with a heart-shaped outline), and rosette (a radiating petal-like design).

Classical antiquity continued to provide a fertile source of inspiration for designers and craftsmen following the American and French revolutions, its moral values being especially welcome during those eras of upheaval (see FEDERAL and EMPIRE), as well as during the English REGENCY and German BIEDERMEIER periods. Late Neoclassical styles persisted to the mid-nineteenth century (see VICTORIAN and SECOND EMPIRE) and reappeared in the twentieth. From shortly after 1900 to the 1930s Neoclassicism, treated in an abstracted manner (see ART DECO), promoted the virtues of simplicity and geometric clarity in reaction to ART NOUVEAU. In the 1970s and 1980s a descriptive, nostalgic form of Neoclassicism was adopted by postmodern architects and designers seeking to enrich their work with historical references.

NEO-GOTHIC—*see* GOTHIC REVIVAL

NÉO-GREC—*see* SECOND EMPIRE

PETER CARL FABERGÉ (1846–1920).
Imperial Basket of Lilies of the Valley, 1896. Russian.
Gold, silver, nephrite, pearls, and diamonds, 7½ x 8½ x 5¾ in.
(19 x 21.9 x 14.6 cm). New Orleans Museum of Art; Matilda Geddings
Gray Foundation Collection.

OBJECTS OF VERTU

As used in the ANTIQUES trade, the term *objects of vertu* (excellence) refers to small, decorative objects, generally made of GOLD AND SILVER, HARDSTONES, and other rare and precious materials. Prized for their skilled workmanship, these include snuffboxes, compacts, powder boxes, needle cases, cheroot cases, cigarette cases, toothpick cases, scent bottles, frames for miniature portraits, pens, and pen rests. Among the best-known objects of vertu are the hardstone STATUETTES of animals, Easter eggs, and sprays of flowers in miniature baskets created by the Russian goldsmith and jeweler Peter Carl Fabergé before the Revolution.

PAPIER-MÂCHÉ

Papier-mâché, a material molded from paper pulp and glue, was introduced toward the end of the eighteenth century for the fabrication of small decorative objects and furniture. The development of papier-mâché (as a substitute for wood) was allied to the craft of japanning (see LACQUER), and the superior surface for lacquerwork that this material provided was as important as its strength and versatility. The papier-mâché trade was centered in the Midlands of England, principally in Birmingham and Wolverhampton. The quality of manufacture and ornamentation found there was never surpassed on the Continent or in the United States (where papier-mâché objects were produced in significant amounts in Litchfield, Connecticut, during the nineteenth century).

A process for making durable papier-mâché panels that would not warp or crack and that could be sawn, planed, and dovetailed was patented in 1772 by Henry Clay of Birmingham, who advertised the panels as suitable for coaches and sedan chairs, interior paneling, cabinetry, furniture, trays, and other such objects. Clay himself was known as a manufacturer of fine furniture and as japanner to the Crown. He made his panels from sheets of paper that were glued and pressed together, then oven dried; these were shaped, lacquered, given many coats of varnish, and then polished to a fine, black, lustrous finish highly suitable for gilding and painting. When Clay's patent expired in 1802, other manufacturers entered the field, which greatly expanded. With the later introduction of direct molding processes, tea trays decorated with floral and all manner of pictorial subjects became the most common objects made from papier-mâché. It was also used for painted furniture, particularly for light side chairs and ladies' worktables. After 1825, when Jennens & Bettridge (the best-known Birmingham papier-mâché manu-

Lady's Worktable, c. 1860. English. Painted and gilded papier-mâché, inlaid with mother-of-pearl, height: 30½ in. (77.5 cm). Philadelphia Museum of Art; The Henry P. McIlhenny Collection in memory of Frances P. McIlhenny.

facturer) patented a technique for inlaying mother-of-pearl, its distinctive iridescence was added to the typically lush decoration characteristic of VIC-TORIAN work in this medium.

PENNSYLVANIA GERMAN

Pennsylvania German (or Dutch, from the German *Deutsch*) is the generic name given to the arts of the many different religious and regional groups who, starting in the late seventeenth century, fled the wars, religious perse-cutions, and economic upheavals of Germanic eastern and northern Europe to settle in Pennsylvania. Highly skilled artisans, these immigrants and their descendants created one of the richest and most clearly identifiable tradi-tions of FOLK ART in America. They liberally decorated their utilitarian objects (even their foodstuffs) as well as their ornamental pieces with an engaging repertoire of distinctive motifs. Especially favored were patterns from their homelands—hearts, flowers (especially tulips), animals, and birds; eagles, soldiers, and groups of figures were added during the Revolutionary War and FEDERAL periods.

Capitalizing on Pennsylvania's abundant natural resources, they devoted themselves to working wood, forging iron, molding pottery, and weaving wool and cotton. Woodworkers made furniture, including massive wardrobes *(Schranks)* of carved and turned natural black walnut (following the north German tradition) or painted pine (in the mode prevalent in south-ern Germany, Alsace, and Switzerland). Wood was also used for small wares such as butter prints, pastry molds, other kitchenware, toys, and larger, purely decorative carvings—notably, the painted eagles by Wilhelm Schimmel. Smiths cut and soldered tin into candle molds, sconces, and cookie cutters. Blacksmiths forged tools, hinges, hasps, and other HARDWARE AND FITTINGS; and they cast waffle irons, kettles, and stove plates ornamented with biblical scenes. Production of ordinary glazed redware pottery was extensive, and presentation pieces were elaborately decorated, using white and colored slips and sgraffito techniques, to inscribe proverbs and humor-ous sayings in English and German. NEEDLEWORK included bedclothes, show (or display) towels, and samplers worked in cross-stitch as well as colorful pieced quilts—a technique borrowed from the communities' Anglo-Saxon neighbors and first taken up around the middle of the nineteenth century.

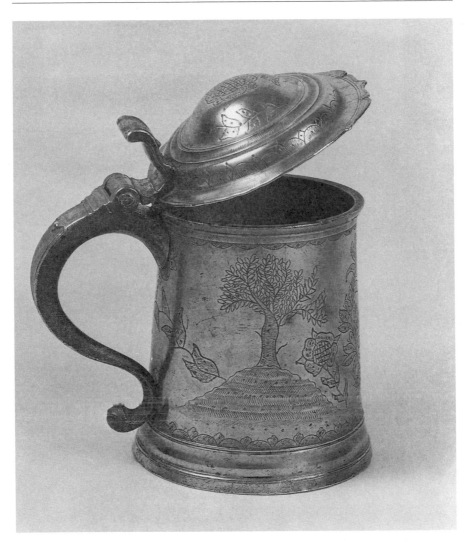

JOHN WILL (C. 1707–1774).
Tankard, 1752–74. American. Pewter, height: 7⅛ in. (18.1 cm).
The Metropolitan Museum of Art, New York; Gift of Mrs. J. Insley Blair
in memory of her husband, J. Insley Blair, 1940.

PEWTER

Like BRONZE, pewter is an alloy of COPPER and TIN, with tin being the principal element. Lesser quality pewter can also contain lead, which makes it cheaper but also darker in color (gray rather than silvery) and unsuitable for use with food. The medieval pewterers guild in England standardized the alloy for pewter as 112 pounds of tin with 26 pounds of copper for flatwares and 26 pounds of lead in place of copper for hollow wares; the guild required marks to be struck on all pewter wares by their makers as a guarantee of quality. From the seventeenth century, English pewterers also used secondary marks, including hallmarks, a rose and crown, and a crowned X, whose meanings are now unclear.

Softer than silver, pewter scratches, dents, breaks easily, and also tarnishes. Articles made of pewter are always cast, as it is neither as malleable nor as resilient as silver or copper. After casting, the objects can be finished on a type of lathe, where the surfaces are planed and casting seams removed. Decoration can be cast in relief with the object or engraved on the surface afterward. Pewter can be polished to a bright finish resembling silver, and it was as a substitute for silver that pewter articles were made in Europe and America, particularly in the seventeenth and eighteenth centuries. These included all manner of household wares, from plates, cups, bowls, and spoons to candlesticks and decorative vessels. From the late sixteenth to the nineteenth century, it remained the principal material for tablewares in prosperous and middle-class households, replaced only in the nineteenth century by ceramics and glass.

PIETRE DURE—*see* HARDSTONES

PORCELAIN

Porcelain, a ceramic body fired at very high temperatures (see POTTERY), is made of a fine white refractory, or heat-resistant, clay (china clay, or kaolin) and feldspar (china stone, or petuntse), which combine under intense heat. True, or hard-paste, porcelain is white, hard, translucent, impermeable to liquids, and resonant when struck. Developed in China about the ninth century A.D., it was admired in the West for its translucency and whiteness, and European potters, lacking knowledge of its composition, attempted to imitate it by mixing lower-firing white clays with ground glass. Such artificial, or soft-paste, porcelains, produced widely in the eighteenth century, are somewhat translucent, porous, and softer and more fragile than true porcelain, fracturing easily. Porcelain is nonporous and can be left in its "biscuit" state (without a vitreous coating or glaze) or glazed with a composition of the same elements as the porcelain body, producing a thin, glittering, homogeneous surface when fired. Porcelain can be decorated under the glaze with such colors as blue (derived from cobalt oxide), which withstand the high temperatures of the kiln (above 1,200 degrees Centigrade), or over the glaze with enamel colors and gilding, which stand out from the surface and are fixed in a separate, lower-firing "muffle" kiln (at 800–900 degrees Centigrade).

By the sixteenth century, Chinese porcelain was a common article of trade in Europe. The first attempts to produce porcelain in Europe took place during the RENAISSANCE at the Medici court in Florence in the 1570s and at Rouen, France, a century later, although the necessary natural materials and the ability to secure and maintain high kiln temperatures were lacking and only a few soft-paste pieces were produced. True hard-paste porcelain was first made successfully at Meissen, Germany, in 1708 by the alchemist Johann Friedrich Böttger, who discovered white china clay in the region. His patron, Elector Augustus the Strong of Saxony, established the royal Saxon porcelain factory at Meissen in 1710, thereafter carefully guarding the secret of porcelain manufacture in order to protect the income it generated as a luxury export trade. Nevertheless, deserters from the factory helped to establish rival manufactories at Vienna (1718) and Venice (1720). From Vienna the secret spread to Doccia, Italy (1737); Nymphenburg (1747), Höchst (1750), Strasbourg (1752), and Frankenthal (1755) in Germany; and elsewhere. Because of the extraordinary inventiveness of its painters and modelers and the extremely high quality of its porcelain, Meissen remained the most important porcelain factory in Europe for some forty years; its products were widely imitated, from the CHINOISERIE landscapes painted by J. G. Héroldt in the largest palette of enamel colors then known to the STATUETTES of human figures, animals, and birds and the sculptural tablewares modeled by J. J. Kändler.

In competition and often under aristocratic protection, soft-paste factories were established all over Europe, making products that were much improved technically over the earlier attempts, though still difficult and expensive to make: in France at Saint-Cloud (1678), Chantilly (1726), Vincennes (later Sèvres) (1738), and Mennecy (1748); in Italy at Capodimonte (1743); in Spain at Buen Retiro (1759); and in England at Bow (1744), Chelsea (1745), and Worcester (1751). Of these, the factory at Sèvres, protected by LOUIS XV and

LOUIS XVI, came to dominate European porcelain markets and fashions, succeeding to the position lost by Meissen during the Seven Years' War (1756–63). Sèvres was famous for its brilliantly colored enamel grounds (royal and turquoise blue, daffodil yellow, apple green, and rose pink, among others), with painted decorations of figures, birds, and flowers set in white reserve panels, and for its lavish use of gilding in the form of floral sprays raised in relief and its delicately tooled pebble and meander patterns. Hard-paste porcelain was made at Sèvres from 1768, gradually replacing the soft-paste production.

In England about 1800, Josiah Spode II introduced bone china, a new, hybrid porcelain that contained bone ash. Dazzlingly white, translucent when thin, and harder than many conventional soft pastes, bone china is somewhat porous and thus usually glazed. Bone china became the standard English commercial porcelain of the nineteenth and twentieth centuries, and it was made also in America, where the first hard-paste porcelains were produced by William Ellis Tucker in Philadelphia from 1825.

POTTERY

Pottery is clay hardened by heat, usually in a kiln. There are many types of pottery, which vary according to the composition of the clay and the temperature at which it is fired. *Pottery* is sometimes used loosely to describe all ceramic wares made from baked clay, including stoneware, which is fired at very high temperatures (1,050–1,200 degrees Centigrade), and PORCELAIN, which is fired at even higher temperatures (becoming semivitreous in the process); but the term is more accurately restricted to ceramic wares fired at the lowest kiln temperatures (800–1,000 degrees Centigrade), which are called "earthenware." Earthenware—which contains a relatively high percentage of iron oxide, which lowers the firing temperature and colors the clays—is typically coarse grained, porous, fragile, and tends to shrink in firing. In order to seal such pottery against penetration by liquids, a vitreous coating known as a "glaze" must be used. When applied to the clay surface and fired in the kiln, the glaze becomes glasslike.

There are two distinct types of low-firing pottery glazes. Lead glaze, which contains lead oxide, produces a thin, translucent, bright, glossy surface in a single firing. It can be colored or stained with metallic oxides (iron for red, copper for green), but it retains its translucency so that decorative designs on the surface of the object—whether painted in different colored clays, incised, or molded in relief—remain visible under the glaze. Lead-glazed

Attributed to **GEORGE HUBENER** (1757–1828).
Dish, 1785–86. Made in Upper Hanover Township, Montgomery
County, Pennsylvania. Slip- and sgraffito-decorated redware,
diameter: 13½ in. (34.2 cm). Philadelphia Museum of Art; Purchased:
Baugh-Barber Fund.

pottery, known since antiquity in the West, was produced extensively until the eighteenth century, when it was largely replaced by more technically sophisticated ceramic bodies and glazes, except in work done in traditional communities (for example, the pottery of the PENNSYLVANIA GERMANS).

European lead-glazed pottery, used in the Middle Ages for tableware, kitchenware, and pharmacy vessels, was often decorated with incised designs or with raised applications of clay. By the RENAISSANCE, improved techniques of manufacture, especially the ability to control kiln temperatures, led to the development of slipware—pottery decorated before the glaze was applied with designs painted in various colored liquid clays, or slips. Slipware could be further decorated with the technique of sgraffito (scratching), in which the surface is covered with slip and designs are produced by incising or even combing through the slip to expose the color of the clay body underneath. RESTORATION potters (Thomas Toft, among them) would apply pads of slip that had designs, letters, or numbers impressed in them with metal dies; in sixteenth-century France, decorations made with this technique were often emblems, monograms, or princely coats-of-arms speckled in lead glazes of green, yellow, and brown. To conceal the dark clay body and provide a light ground for polychrome decoration, many lead-glazed wares were initially coated with white slip.

Tin glaze, another low-firing pottery glaze, contains tin oxide, which when fired produces a dense, opaque white surface that also masks the underlying clay. Tin-glazed wares can be decorated with pigments containing metallic oxides—cobalt for blue, manganese for purple, copper for green, and iron for red—"high-temperature colors" that withstand the heat of the glaze firing. They can also be decorated with lower-firing metallic pigments known as "enamels," which include a wider, if more fragile, range of colors. These are applied over the once-fired tin glaze and fixed in a second low-temperature firing, a technique introduced in the eighteenth century. When fired on top of the tin glaze under reducing (oxygen-depriving) conditions, certain metallic pigments develop unique color characteristics and produce an iridescent metallic surface known as "luster," a technique that spread from the Near East to Spain in the Middle Ages (see HISPANO-MORESQUE).

Rivaling the white, glassy porcelain being imported from China during the Renaissance and BAROQUE periods, tin-glazed earthenwares with painted decorations were produced in most European countries, where they were known by different names: majolica in Italy; faience in France; Delft in Holland; and delftware in England. Styles of decoration varied regionally and with shifts in politics and taste. One style nearly universal in northern

Europe from the sixteenth to the eighteenth century imitated Chinese patterns in blue and white; it was most strongly developed at Delft, in Holland, where TILES—used on walls in kitchens and dairies, as skirting in living rooms, and as fireplace surrounds—were made and widely exported. Several pottery centers in Renaissance Italy, among them Orvieto, Urbino, and Faenza, specialized in multicolored *istoriato* (narrative) decorations inspired by contemporary engravings, such as those painted by Francesco Xanto Avelli in Urbino about 1530. Lusterwares were made at Deruta and Gubbio, the latter being famous for its range of gold, ruby red, and silver colors.

Starting in the Middle Ages, especially in Germany, the production of earthenware was rivaled by that of stoneware—a hard, dense, opaque pottery that is nonporous and fires at higher temperatures. Stonewares can be left unglazed but are frequently salt-glazed: salt is thrown into the kiln at the height of the firing, and as the salt vaporizes, the sodium in it combines with components of the clay to form a thin, hard, colorless glaze with a characteristic pitted, orange-peel texture. By the late seventeenth and early eighteenth centuries, potters in England, Holland, and Germany were producing fine-grained, unglazed red stonewares that could be finished to a mat surface; they were decorated with molded sprigs of flowers and leaves in imitation of the Chinese red stonewares then being imported to Europe along with tea.

The introduction of vessels for tea, coffee, and chocolate and the development of large table services complete with tureens, centerpieces, and various dishes in the eighteenth and early nineteenth centuries in Europe and America spurred the widespread importation of Chinese porcelains (see EXPORT WARES), whose relatively low cost rivaled that of pottery. In the mid-eighteenth century in Staffordshire, England, a fine cream-colored, lead-glazed earthenware that compared to porcelain was introduced. Because of its low cost and pleasing designs—especially those by the firm of Josiah Wedgwood, which were exported to Europe in large quantities—creamware largely drove other earthenwares as well as porcelains from the market. Sturdy and simple to decorate, creamware lent itself to the new process of transfer printing and other decorative techniques. In transfer printing, a print is made on paper and immediately pressed against the surface of a piece of pottery, leaving a monochrome impression, like an engraving, that can be overpainted. In the nineteenth century, independent artist-potters and pottery firms sought to rediscover and revive historical techniques of pottery manufacture and decoration, including painted majolica, which was made both in Europe and America in the RENAISSANCE REVIVAL style, and Asian-style wares and their glazes, which were imitated by ART NOUVEAU designers.

BENJAMIN PYNE (active 1676–1732)
and **PETER ARCHAMBO** (active 1721–67).
Kettle, Cream Pitcher, and Sugar Box, 1720–22. English.
Silver and wood, kettle height: 7⅝ in. (19.4 cm); creamer height:
5¾ in. (14.6 cm); sugar box height: 4¼ in. (10.8 cm). Philadelphia
Museum of Art; Gift of Mrs. Widener Dixon and George D. Widener.

QUEEN ANNE

▷ **WHO** ARCHITECTS: Nicholas Hawksmoor, Sir John Vanbrugh
CRAFTSMEN AND MANUFACTURERS: John Ody, William Old, Simon Pantin, John Phillips, Pierre Platel, Benjamin Pyne, Thomas Roberts, David Willaume I

▷ **WHEN** 1702 to 1714

▷ **WHERE** England and America

▷ **WHAT** Extending through the reign of Queen Anne (1702–14) and well into the GEORGIAN period in England and the American colonies, the court style known as Queen Anne continued the course of design established under WILLIAM AND MARY, an international BAROQUE style dependent on foreign trade and the influence of French Huguenot and Dutch craftsmen. But a growing emphasis placed on form rather than rich surface ornamentation led to a new discipline, restraint, and a simple elegance of design throughout the decorative arts. In furniture, the gently curving cabriole leg ending in a hoof, paw, or club foot, introduced from the Continent at the beginning of the century (see RÉGENCE), was eventually appended to virtually every type of furniture, from walnut cabinets with figured veneers to fire screens and upholstered wing chairs. From cabriole legs to cresting rail, the serpentine side chair with its new vase or fiddle-shaped back splat demonstrated the principle of contrasted curves that was widely adopted during the period and best defines the style. Queen Anne silver introduced new, simply decorated and utilitarian domestic forms—pear-shaped teapots, straight-sided coffeepots with graceful spouts—for the serving of beverages from the East, but show silver could still be elaborately engraved in the style of French Régence designs.

In the late nineteenth century, the so-called Queen Anne Revival spurred an interest in early-eighteenth-century antiques and the manufacture of reproductions of them. However, following the pattern of many other revival styles, objects made in the name of Queen Anne often had only vague connections to authentic period forms (see AESTHETIC MOVEMENT) other than a preference for formal and decorative restraint.

QUEEN ANNE REVIVAL—*see* AESTHETIC MOVEMENT

RÉGENCE

▷ **WHO** ARCHITECTS, ARTISTS, AND DESIGNERS: Claude III Audran, Jean Berain, Robert de Cotte, Claude Gillot, Gilles-Marie Oppenord, Bernard Toro, François-Antoine Vassé, Antoine Watteau
CRAFTSMEN AND MANUFACTURERS: Claude II Ballin, Nicolas Besnier, Charles Cressent, Nicolas Delaunay

▷ **WHEN** 1715 to 1723

▷ **WHERE** France

▷ **WHAT** *Régence* is the name given to the transitional style between BAROQUE and ROCOCO that flourished in France during the regency (1715–23) of Philippe, duc d'Orléans, although it actually began during the reign of LOUIS XIV and ended after LOUIS XV came of age. It is generally characterized by a light and delicate treatment of architectural forms and ornament, with finely carved wood paneling *(boiseries)* and reliefs, often painted in white and gold, replacing the geometric compartments and densely colored marbles and mythological paintings that typically covered BAROQUE walls and ceilings. The decorative schemes that Gilles-Marie Oppenord created for the regent at the Palais Royal in Paris (c. 1720) made him a central figure in the development of the Régence style. They included delicate, shallow, grotesque ornament inspired by the engraved designs of Claude III Audran and Claude Gillot as well as new motifs, including bat wings, naturalistic plants, and the *espagnolette* (a mask in a stylized shell). Furniture designers also moved away from the grand, heavy forms and somber coloring of earlier work, such as André-Charles Boulle's, toward pieces that were lighter in color and design.

Typical of the Régence style is the furniture of Charles Cressent, with its serpentine shapes and naturalistic, sometimes asymmetrical decorations in gilded metal and colored marquetries. The commodes "à la Régence" produced by Cressent were light, with tall, slender, curving legs, serpentine front, and two tiers of drawers that contrasted with the massive three-tiered chests on very short legs that had been made at the turn of the century. The sculptural quality of Cressent's furniture mounts and his use of shell, vegetal, and animal forms, some inspired by Antoine Watteau's paintings, reflect a trend toward naturalism that prefigured the Rococo. Naturalism appeared also in dress silks, which represented flowers and foliage, some so closely spaced as to suggest a field of wildflowers. Still rectilinear and symmetrical during the period of Louis XIV, Régence design evolved toward the asymmetry, complexity, and movement that characterized design under Louis XV.

Armchair, c. 1710–20. Made in Paris. Gilded walnut and leather, height: 43¾ in. (111 cm). Musée du Louvre, Paris; Gift of Comte Robert-Henry de Caumont La Force.

PAUL STORR (1771–1844).
Tureen, 1805–6. English. Silver, height: 14¼ in. (36 cm). The Royal Collection of Her Majesty Queen Elizabeth II, London.

REGENCY

▷ **WHO** ARCHITECTS AND DESIGNERS: Rudolph Ackermann, George Bullock, John Crace, Henry Holland, Thomas Hope, John Nash, George Smith CRAFTSMEN AND MANUFACTURERS: Rundell, Bridge & Rundell; Paul Storr

▷ **WHEN** 1811 to 1820

▷ **WHERE** Great Britain

▷ **WHAT** *Regency* is loosely applied to NEOCLASSICISM in Britain from the 1790s to the 1830s, although the term strictly refers to the period of the regency (1811–20) of George Augustus Frederick, Prince of Wales, who in 1820 succeeded his father as King George IV (reigned 1820–30). Like the EMPIRE style in France to which it was most indebted initially, Regency design was monumental, distinguished by solid forms, boldly scaled ornaments, and archaeological detail. The French character of the Regency style followed changing fashion from LOUIS XVI to Empire, as illustrated in *Household Furniture and Interior Decoration* (1807) by Thomas Hope, who was an admirer of Charles Percier and Pierre-François-Léonard Fontaine. Intended to provide models for designers and craftsmen, Hope's collection of designs included a highly personal mixture of archaeological styles—Greek, Roman, and Egyptian—that emphasized straight lines, bold curves, and broad, uninterrupted surfaces. The furniture types that Hope popularized—a circular table with a single pedestal support and the Greek *klismos* chair with saber shaped legs—typified the forms that spread to America as the Greek Revival style. Hope's designs were circulated by George Smith, whose own pattern book, *A Collection of Designs for Household Furniture and Interior Decoration* (1808), was also influential in spreading the Regency style. His designs were largely Grecian, but Smith also introduced picturesque and exotic elements, such as Gothic and Chinese styles, into the Regency vocabulary, claiming, for example, that Gothic produced "a more abundant variety of ornaments and forms" than any other style. This taste for the nonclassical (non-Western) and the romantic distinguished English design in the first decades of the nineteenth century, as it had in the eighteenth (see GEORGIAN). It was promoted by the prince regent in his Chinese Rooms at Carlton House in London designed by Henry Holland (1788–90; see CHINOISERIE) and in the Royal Pavilion at Brighton, which John Nash rebuilt in an Indian style with domes, pierced stonework lattice screens, and cast-iron palm-tree columns (1815–21).

The widening stylistic base of Regency was demonstrated in Smith's *Cabinet-Maker and Upholsterer's Guide* (1826), which illustrated Neoclassical, GOTHIC REVIVAL, and LOUIS XIV interiors, and in England's leading design magazine, Rudolph Ackermann's *Repository of Arts* (1809–28). The *Repository* first included Greek designs after Hope and Percier and Fontaine, but from the mid-1820s featured Gothic designs by A. C. Pugin. In metalwork, ceramics, and textiles, classical forms and ornaments also came to coexist with romantic and exotic ones. Paul Storr created silver-gilt wine coolers in the form of the Roman "Warwick" vase for the prince regent as well as highly ROCOCO silver-gilt pieces, which were used in the French and Chinese interiors at Carlton House and Brighton. Also, women's clothing ranged from high-waisted Empire-style dresses with plain bodices and narrow skirts that fell straight and close to the figure in the fashion of Greek draperies to Elizabethan ruffs and Moorish turbans.

RELIGIOUS OBJECTS

Often the forms and styles of religious articles follow so closely those of secular production that only the presence of a symbol or inscription, their provenance, or the documentation of use reveals their ritual associations. Some objects, however, are specific to the liturgy and regulated by a distinctive tradition established early in the history of the faith, such as the vestments worn by the Catholic clergy, many of which are based on ancient Roman dress. Ecclesiastical objects have come on the market over the centuries because of ideological upheavals, persecution, the closing of churches, changes in taste, and unauthorized sales, as well as thievery.

Christian liturgical objects pertain mainly to the furnishing of the church and altar and the celebration of Communion. They were more or less elaborately decorated depending on their period and the sect for which they were made; during the RENAISSANCE, altar linens were made of silks and brocades embroidered with figures and scenes, whereas ROCOCO floral patterns were preferred in the eighteenth century. Eucharistic articles include the chalices for the wine and patens, or plates, for holding the wafer; cruets, for wine or water; and pyxes and monstrances for displaying the Consecrated Host. During the Middle Ages these were often made of enameled copper, but later they were customarily fashioned of gold or silver, with embossed and engraved ornamentation. Anglican communion silver, on the contrary, was generally simple in shape and spare in decoration.

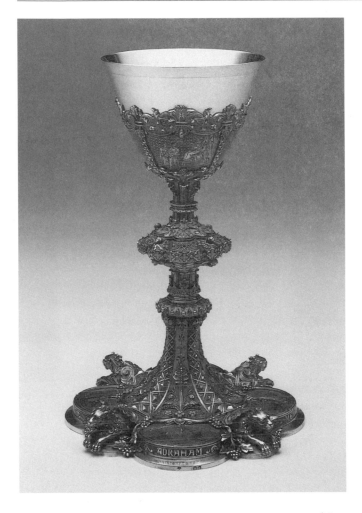

THOMAS-JOSEPH ARMAND-CALLIAT (1822–1901).
Chalice, c. 1870. French. Silver gilt and enamel, height: 10½ in.
(26.7 cm). Philadelphia Museum of Art; Gift of the Friends of
the Museum.

In the nineteenth century such influential architects as A. W. N. Pugin in England (in *The True Principles of Pointed or Christian Architecture,* 1843) and Eugène-Emmanuel Viollet-le-Duc in France associated the Christian faith with the Gothic style, which they practiced during a period of intense restoration of medieval religious architecture and construction of new churches. Appropriate furnishings of ivory, gold and silver, bronze, and needlework in GOTHIC REVIVAL styles were created for these buildings, many designed by their architects. Manufacturers specialized in this market. John Hardman's Birmingham factory began by making "medieval" metalwork to Pugin's designs in 1838 and then expanded its production to embroideries, stained glass, carvings, and other church articles. In Paris, Placide Poussielgue-Rusand used industrial techniques and catalog-marketing methods to bring precious- and base-metal versions of his commissions in the Gothic style to a broad ecclesiastical market.

Jewish ceremonial objects (see JUDAICA) relate more often to the home (where the celebration of the Sabbath and other holidays was focused) than the synagogue, although rich furnishings were created for the housing and dressing of the Torah scrolls—notably silver crowns, finials, breastplates, and pointers, as well as embroidered Torah binders and mantles, and curtains for the Holy Ark. Like Christian liturgical objects, those used for Jewish rituals often followed the prevailing styles of the communities in which they were made, but in the nineteenth century they too experienced a historicizing period, when Moorish architecture became popular for synagogues, and casts and copies were made of fourteenth-century Spanish, French, and Italian Hanukkah menorahs.

RENAISSANCE

▷ **WHO** ARCHITECTS, ARTISTS, AND DESIGNERS: Leon Battista Alberti, Sebald Beham, Giovanni Bologna, Cornelis Bos, René Boyvin, Donato Bramante, Agnolo Bronzino, Filippo Brunelleschi, Jean Cousin, Philibert Delorme, Donatello, Jacques Androuet Du Cerceau, Albrecht Dürer, Cornelis II Floris, Peter Flötner, Jean Goujon, Nicholas Hilliard, Hans Holbein, Leonardo da Vinci, Leone Leoni, Pompeo Leoni, Pierre Lescot, Masaccio, Michelangelo Buonarotti, Bernard Palissy, Andrea Palladio, Germain Pilon, Jacopo Pontormo, Francesco Primaticcio, Marcantonio Raimondi, Raphael, Giulio Romano, Rosso Fiorentino, Francesco Salviati, Hugues Sambin, Sebastiano Serlio, Pietro Torrigiano, Agostino Veneziano, Enea Vico, Hans Vredeman de Vries

CRAFTSMEN AND MANUFACTURERS: Benvenuto Cellini, Etienne Delaune, Andrea della Robbia, Giovanni della Robbia, Luca della Robbia, Lorenzo Ghiberti, Erasmus Hornick, Wenzel Jamnitzer, Elias Lencker, Jakob Mores

▷ **WHEN** 1400 to 1600

▷ **WHERE** Europe

▷ **WHAT** *Renaissance,* meaning "rebirth," has been used since the sixteenth century to describe the revival of classical art and literature that began in Florence during the fifteenth century and continued in Rome. It was spread across Italy and Europe by itinerant artists and craftsmen and by the pattern books and engraved designs that became available after the invention of printing about 1450. The style was advanced by the patronage of the wealthiest European courts—those of the Medici in Florence, the papacy in Rome, Francis I in France, Henry VIII in England, and the Holy Roman emperors Charles V in the Netherlands, Spain, and Germany and Rudolf II in Prague. The Renaissance took its visual forms and ornamental motifs largely from Roman architecture and sculpture; from the classical orders with their columns, capitals, and enrichments (particularly acanthus leaves); and from sarcophagi, triumphal arches, and other antique monuments decorated with human and mythological figures, trophies of arms, and naturalistic wreaths and swags. From Roman wall paintings and stucco decorations discovered in buried ancient ruins, or "grottoes," Renaissance artists borrowed so-called grotesque compositions of vases, candelabra, vegetal scrolls, masks, and chimerical monsters, which they arranged in vertical panels. Antique furniture forms were also revived, including the X-frame Roman magistrate's chair *(sella curulis),* both with and without a back, and the Roman table with fan-shaped, slab uprights *(cartibulum)* elaborately carved with grotesque creatures, human half-figures, and confronted animals. Characteristic of the Renaissance wherever it appeared was an interest in the human figure, whether painted on furniture or ceramics, carved in wood, or cast in metal.

The Renaissance is generally distinguished by solid, sculptural, heroic forms; realistically observed details; and balanced, symmetrical compositions ordered by mathematically determined proportional relationships, but it did admit much regional variety and could be intensely individual. The creators of the Italian Renaissance were famous for their multiple skills: Lorenzo Ghiberti trained as a goldsmith, qualified as a painter, practiced as a sculptor, and designed stained glass and ecclesiastical vestments; Leonardo—a virtuoso of such fantastic range that he impressed even his contemporaries—was active as a painter, sculptor, engineer, anatomist, and natural scientist; Raphael, who practiced architecture and painting, also designed metalware and TAPESTRIES; and Michelangelo was a painter, sculptor, and architect regarded as almost without peer. Their work was widely circulated in engravings, providing models for craftsmen. Prints after Raphael—for example, those by Marcantonio Raimondi—were copied on many different types of objects, including Italian majolica (see POTTERY) made at such centers as Urbino and Faenza, and French ENAMELS from Limoges.

About 1520 Michelangelo, Agnolo Bronzino, Jacopo Pontormo, Giulio Romano, and other artists developed a late form of Renaissance known as Mannerism. This decorative, self-conscious style deliberately violated the stability and order of Renaissance composition with its figures in bizarre and convoluted poses, irrational and unpredictable dispositions of space, discordant colors, and rich, often illusionistic ornaments. It was largely in the form of Mannerism that the Renaissance style traveled abroad. After the sack of Rome in 1527 by the armies of Emperor Charles V, a number of artists left Rome. Among them were Rosso Fiorentino and Francesco Primaticcio, who went to France to work for FRANCIS I on the decoration of the château of Fontainebleau. Even more influential than their paintings were the ornamental stucco frames that Rosso invented, with bands of strapwork (leatherlike scrolls that appear to have been cut and rolled by hand) combined with human figures. The Fontainebleau decorations, published by René Boyvin and others, inspired Cornelis Bos, Cornelis II Floris, and Hans Vredeman de Vries in the Netherlands to engrave their own strapwork designs, which spread the style throughout northern Europe and were included among the sources used by decorative plasterers in Elizabethan England (see TUDOR).

While Italian artists worked in the north—Pietro Torrigiano in England in the 1510s, Benvenuto Cellini and Sebastiano Serlio in France in the 1540s, and Leone and Pompeo Leoni in Spain from the 1550s—northern artists, most notably Albrecht Dürer, traveled to Italy. Famed for his paintings and engravings, Dürer also supplied designs to goldsmiths.

RENAISSANCE REVIVAL

▷ **WHO** ARCHITECTS, ARTISTS, AND DESIGNERS: Charles Barry, Albert-Ernest Carrier-Belleuse, Aimé Chenavard, Ludwig Grüner, Emile Jeannest, Jean-Baptiste-Jules Klagmann, Alexandre-Eugène Prignot, Gottfried Semper, Alfred Stevens
CRAFTSMEN AND MANUFACTURERS: Léon Arnoux; Charles-Jean Avisseau; Elkington, Mason & Co.; Fannière Frères; Jacques-Henri Fauconnier;

ALEXANDRE-GEORGES FOURDINOIS (1799–1871).
Cabinet, 1855. French. Walnut, 117 x 50 x 24 in.
(297.2 x 127 x 61 cm). Victoria and Albert Museum, London.

Alexandre-Georges Fourdinois; Henri-Auguste Fourdinois; François-Désiré Froment-Meurice; Emile Froment-Meurice; Luigi Frullini; Holland & Sons; Hunt & Roskell; Jackson & Graham; Minton & Co.; Léonard Moreil-Ladeuil; Antonio Salviati; Antoine Vechte; Jules-Claude Ziegler

▷ **WHEN** 1830s through 1880s

▷ **WHERE** Europe and the United States

▷ **WHAT** The Renaissance Revival first appeared in architecture during the 1820s with the adoption of Italian sixteenth-century villas and palaces as models for secular buildings such as clubs, offices, town halls, and houses. It ran parallel to the GOTHIC REVIVAL and shared some of that style's taste for picturesque effects, although lacking its moral overtones and ecclesiastical applications. The subsequent adoption of the Renaissance style for decorative and useful wares typically involved Italian forms, like the painted tin-enameled POTTERY made by Minton in the styles of sixteenth-century Italian majolica of the Urbino region and the colored glasswares with filigree GLASS canes and elaborate pincered trailing in the manner of sixteenth- and seventeenth-century Venetian glass, made by firms as varied as those of Antonio Salviati and the Compagnia di Venezia e Murano in Venice, Carl Florenz Heinrich Müller in Hamburg, the Rheinischen Glashütten in Cologne, and Hodgetts, Richardson & Son in Stourbridge, England.

The Renaissance Revival was, however, by no means exclusively Italian in its sources. Like the Gothic Revival, it was also nationalistic. In France, firms such as those of the Fourdinois family revived the sixteenth-century style of FRANCIS I, with large, two-tiered walnut cupboards carved with sculptural decoration; Charles-Jean Avisseau and others modeled lead-glazed earthenwares in plant and animal forms in the style of the sixteenth-century pottery maker Bernard Palissy; and Jules Brateau adapted the Mannerist PEWTER wares of François Briot. In Austria the goldsmith Hermann Ratzersdorfer created standing cups of rock crystal and enamel mounted in silver gilt that resembled the court treasures of Rudolf II; in Italy the furniture maker Luigi Frullini used sixteenth-century-style Italian grotesque figures and animals to decorate furniture for clients at home and abroad, including a commission for the dining room and library at Château-sur-Mer in Newport, Rhode Island. Some sources were closely reproduced, but others were often freely interpreted in both style and medium. Minton, for example, produced what appeared to be Limoges ENAMELS on bone china and replicated inlaid Saint-Porchaire earthenwares with painted as well as inlaid decorations.

In the United States, the Renaissance Revival reached its height at the Centennial Exhibition in Philadelphia in 1876; strapwork patterns embellished with oval and rectangular panels and cabochons were loosely adapted to massive furniture forms and metalwork. However, with its flat surface decoration of marquetry, paneling, and incised lines, American Renaissance furniture owed more to modern machine techniques and current English reform styles (see AESTHETIC MOVEMENT) than it did to the sixteenth century. In England the Italian Renaissance manner was fostered from about 1850 by Ludwig Grüner and Gottfried Semper (two Germans in the circle of Prince Albert) and by the artist Alfred Stevens. Semper and Stevens exercised particular influence at the Government School of Design (later the Royal College of Art) in London, where they taught; Semper later spread the style in German-speaking countries when he moved to Zurich and Vienna. Although widely admired for its rich effects of color and sculptural detail, the Renaissance Revival style was abjured by design reformers of the ARTS AND CRAFTS MOVEMENT for its lack of simplicity and social purpose.

REPRODUCTIONS—*see* REVIVALS AND REPRODUCTIONS

RESTAURATION—*see* CHARLES X

RESTORATION

▷ **WHO** CRAFTSMEN AND MANUFACTURERS: John Dwight, John Philip Elers, Grinling Gibbons, Francis Poyntz, Daniel Quare, George Ravenscroft, Thomas Toft, Thomas Tompion

▷ **WHEN** 1660 to 1688

▷ **WHERE** England

▷ **WHAT** *Restoration* refers to the return of the Stuarts to the throne of England under Charles II (reigned 1660–85) and James II (reigned 1685–88) after the collapse of the Commonwealth in 1660 (see JACOBEAN). Changes in style rarely coincide as closely with political developments as the change that occurred at this time, when BAROQUE exuberance quickly replaced Puritan austerity. The Restoration period (also called Carolian, after *Carolus*, Latin for Charles) was markedly international, the nobility having returned from exile with Continental ideas about fashion and a heightened taste for stylish imported goods—furniture, velvets and silks, and LACE (prohibited to protect English lace makers but widely smuggled and openly worn; imported Flemish lace was deceptively called *point d'Angleterre,* or English lace, to suggest a native origin). Numerous goods also arrived through lucrative trade with the East, particularly objects of PORCELAIN and of LACQUER, which was imitated by a developing English japanning trade. Printed and painted chintzes imported from India (which after 1662 were mostly EXPORT WARES based on modified Indian patterns in the English taste sent for manufacture there by the East India Company) were themselves also imitated, notably in the popular tree-of-life NEEDLEWORK designs for crewelwork bed hangings and curtains.

Furnishings in great households became luxurious and ostentatious, with opulent use of gilding and silver garnitures (mantel ornaments), mirrors, toilet sets, mounts for fireplace tools, and even furniture (see GOLD AND SILVER). Ornamentation was richly elaborate, from Grinling Gibbons's paneling and mirror frames carved with cherubs and naturalistic swags of fruits and flowers to the carved, pierced, and gilded stands created for lacquer and japanned cabinets and the embossed floral and CHINOISERIE designs on pewter and silver. Continental influence, principally from Holland, came with immigrant craftsmen. They introduced heavily decorated silver, distinctive furniture forms, and veneering and floral marquetry (see FURNITURE) with light, exotic, and colored woods, used on cabinets and the tall cases of the newly invented pendulum clocks. Walnut, now favored for furniture, was given ingenious twisted turnings, which formed the legs of cabinets, tables, and stools, and the legs and uprights of chairs with tall carved backs, often upholstered in cane. GLASS manufacture expanded with the production of lead crystal by George Ravenscroft for tableware about 1674 (soon taken up by glasshouses throughout the country) and of mirror glass by the Vauxhall glasshouse, founded by the second duke of Buckingham about 1663. Outstanding early examples of the developing Staffordshire POTTERY industry were large, slip-decorated plates by such craftsmen as Thomas Toft and the stoneware vessels and salt-glazed figures by John Dwight. Needlework flourished under the Stuarts, from the courtly heraldic designs and lavish church vestments made by professionals to clothing and household furnishings decorated in crewelwork by semiprofessionals and amateurs and naive samplers and stumpwork embroidered by young girls and then made into mirror frames, cases, and jewel boxes.

RESTORATION—*see* CONDITION

REVIVALS AND REPRODUCTIONS

Artists and craftsmen of many cultures have relied on the past for inspiration—reinterpreting, reviving, and reproducing earlier styles. The Romans copied the Greeks, and in turn, artists and designers of the RENAISSANCE and NEOCLASSICISM depended on antiquity for their models. In the nineteenth century the enthusiasm for history and for traditional values led to widespread eclecticism, particularly in the VICTORIAN and SECOND EMPIRE periods, which borrowed heavily from Egypt (see EMPIRE), the Middle Ages (see GOTHIC REVIVAL), and the Renaissance and the eighteenth century (see RENAISSANCE REVIVAL and ROCOCO REVIVAL). Nationalistic and folk revival movements also emerged, including those in Scandinavia and in the United States (see COLONIAL REVIVAL).

The term *revival* suggests borrowing that can be interpretive as well as imitative. Details may be faithfully reproduced from original examples or from engravings, but the scale, material, manufacturing method, and emphasis of revival styles are often altered, resulting in works that speak as much of their own periods as of the past. *Reproductions* are modern copies of earlier works or styles (although, like revival works, they too can reveal their more recent origins). Reproducing French eighteenth-century royal furnishings from museum pieces as well as creating pastiches in the earlier style was a lucrative business in Paris during the later nineteenth century, when a snobbish preference for aristocratic associations continued to favor the ROCOCO as the preferred style for wealthy individuals. A number of highly respected firms in Paris specialized in fine reproduction furniture and bronzes for an international clientele, among them Georges Aix, Alfred Beurdeley, Henri Dasson, Paul Sormani, and Joseph-Emmanuel Zwiener. At the same time, in England, cabinetmakers including Holland & Sons revived eighteenth-century English styles.

In the United States at the beginning of this century, the Colonial Revival inspired a great output of reproduction furnishings, some of it based on examples with patriotic associations, such as pieces used by George and Martha Washington. The Grand Rapids, Michigan, factories were major producers, using mass-production techniques. Other pieces were individually made, following traditional hand craftsmanship. These included works by Wallace Nutting, whose copies produced between 1917 and the late 1930s were based on antique models, and those by Kittinger, which reproduced museum pieces on license from Colonial Williamsburg beginning in 1936.

ROCOCO

▷ **WHO** ARCHITECTS, ARTISTS, AND DESIGNERS: Jacques-François Blondel, Germain Boffrand, François Boucher, Henry Copland, François de Cuvilliés I, Martin Engelbrecht, Etienne-Maurice Falconet, Jean-Honoré Fragonard, Ange-Jacques Gabriel, Hubert-François (Bourguignon) Gravelot, Johann Georg Hertel the Elder, Thomas Johnson, Jacques de LaJoue, Matthias Lock, Juste-Aurèle Meissonnier, Balthasar Neumann, Gilles-Marie Oppenord, Nicolas Pineau, Louis-François Roubiliac, Antoine Watteau
CRAFTSMEN AND MANUFACTURERS: Thomas Affleck, Beauvais tapestry factory, Gousse Bonnin, Bow porcelain factory, Jacques Caffiéri, Chelsea porcelain factory, Thomas Chippendale, Paul Crespin, Derby porcelain factory, Antoine-Robert Gaudreaux, Thomas Germain, Johann Christian Hoppenhaupt, Johann Michael Hoppenhaupt, Paul de Lamerie, John Linnell, Meissen porcelain factory, George Morris, Benjamin Randolph, James Reynolds, Sèvres porcelain factory, Nicholas Sprimont, Philip Syng Jr., Bernard II Van Risen Burgh, George Wickes, Worcester porcelain factory

▷ **WHEN** 1720s through 1770s

▷ **WHERE** Europe and America

▷ **WHAT** The Rococo style originated in France in the second quarter of the eighteenth century and spread throughout Europe and to America by means of engraved designs and pattern books, imported objects, and immigrant craftsmen. Its name (which was not used until the end of the eighteenth century) was derived from the word *rocaille,* designating the rock- and shell-work used to decorate garden grottoes, which became the style's principal ornamental motifs. Known originally as the "picturesque style" *(genre pittoresque),* the Rococo featured such devices as asymmetry, counterbalancing curves of complicated scrollwork (particularly C-scrolls and S-scrolls), and an array of fantastic naturalistic ornaments. Breaking all rules of classical order and symmetry, Rococo designers favored effects of movement, irregularity, and playful unconventionality. They introduced designs with Chinese and (in England) Gothic elements (see CHINOISERIE and GOTHIC REVIVAL) that fed a new taste for the exotic and picturesque.

In contrast to the massive forms and dense, rich ornament of the BAROQUE style, Rococo decoration was most often light and delicate, in color as well as shape. Its principal exponent in France was Juste-Aurèle Meissonnier, whose published designs for objects and interiors popularized asymmetry and displayed an advanced and widely influential vocabulary of scrolls, rockwork, shellwork, fountains, waterfalls, cartouches, and vases. Rococo furniture was contorted into serpentine forms, with curving (cabriole) legs and undulating (bombé) fronts for chests of drawers, sometimes inlaid with delicate floral marquetries (see FURNITURE) or decorated with metal mounts that repeated the scrolling curves of the furniture frames. In architecture, Jacques-François Blondel encouraged the use of smaller and more intimate rooms and garden buildings that were unified in their interior decoration. Nicolas Pineau and Germain Boffrand conceived interiors in which the wall decoration of carving, painting, sculpture, and plasterwork concealed the structural elements, as in Boffrand's oval salons in the Hôtel Soubise in Paris, which were copied by François de Cuvilliés I, architect to the Bavarian court, in the Amalienburg Pavilion at Schloss Nymphenburg in Munich. Although based on French models, the German Rococo was bolder and more idiosyncratic than its counterpart in France. It was also a more wholly interpenetrating style, applied to interior and exterior architecture as well as to furnishings.

The Rococo style was less widely adopted in England, although it was English pattern books and artists that spread the style to America. Known as the "modern" or "modern French" style, English Rococo was developed by immigrant artists such as Gravelot, who published ornamental prints and whose naturalistic ornament combined with curvilinear scrollwork appeared in designs for silver and porcelain. Native artists including Thomas Johnson, Matthias Lock, and John Linnell similarly applied naturalistic ornaments, using flowers, foliage, and aquatic fantasies as the principal decorative motifs for furniture and furnishings. The main Rococo furniture pattern book, Thomas CHIPPENDALE's *Gentleman and Cabinet-Maker's Director* (1754), provided patterns for furniture in the "Gothic, Chinese, and Modern Taste," including chairs with elaborately scrolled and fretted backs.

While American Rococo furniture is popularly called "Chippendale," Chippendale's was only one of several English Rococo pattern books to cross the Atlantic in the eighteenth century. Philadelphia was America's most important center for Rococo, due in part to the many immigrant craftsmen there, including Thomas Affleck, Nicholas Bernard, Gousse Bonnin, Hercules Courtenay, Martin Jugiez, James Reynolds, and Philip Syng Jr. By the time Rococo first took hold in America, around 1750, the style was already under intense criticism in France, for its lack of order, its visual chaos and confusion, and its frivolity compared to the "noble simplicity" of NEOCLASSICISM, which had already begun to supplant it.

Centerpiece, 1893. Made by the Ohio Valley China Company, Wheeling, West Virginia. Bisque-fired and glazed porcelain, height: 25¼ in. (64.1 cm). Philadelphia Museum of Art; Gift of the Ohio Valley China Company.

ROCOCO REVIVAL

▷ **WHO** CRAFTSMEN AND MANUFACTURERS: Léon Arnoux, John Henry Belter, Berlin porcelain factory, Charles Christofle, Coalbrookdale porcelain factory, Cristalleries de Baccarat, Henri Dasson, Derby porcelain factory, G. R. Elkington, Alexandre-Georges Fourdinois, François-Désiré Froment-Meurice, Gillow & Co., Haviland porcelain factory, Höchst porcelain factory, Holland & Sons, Georges-Alphonse Jacob-Desmalter, Charles-Joseph-Marie Jeanselme, Joseph-Pierre-François Jeanselme, Meissen porcelain factory, Minton & Co., Léonard Morel-Ladeuil, Julien-Nicolas Rivart, Rockingham pottery and porcelain factory, Alexander Roux, Sèvres porcelain factory, Benjamin Smith Jr., Antoine Vechte, Worcester porcelain factory

▷ **WHEN** 1830s through 1870s

▷ **WHERE** Europe and the United States

▷ **WHAT** The ROCOCO was the most popularly accepted of the historic styles reintroduced during the mid-nineteenth century (see REVIVALS AND REPRODUCTIONS), having a charm and sensuality that were lacking in the more serious, intellectualized products of NEOCLASSICISM and of the GOTHIC REVIVAL. Called the *"style Pompadour"* in France, and "Old French" or "Louis XIV" in England (where it was made up of both BAROQUE and Rococo elements), the Rococo Revival was aristocratic in origin but was soon favored by middle-class arrivistes as well. It has never completely gone out of fashion. The taste remains today in a plethora of period adaptations and reproductions and in the continuing market for French eighteenth-century objects.

The first signs of the Rococo Revival emerged during the 1820s and 1830s in England, with the painted and gilded French-style paneled interiors designed by Benjamin Dean Wyatt, and in France, under LOUIS-PHILIPPE, with the king's policy of restoring earlier buildings in their appropriate historical styles. These earliest revival interiors in England were fitted out with original seventeenth- and eighteenth-century furniture, which had come on the market after the French Revolution, and were complemented with modern Rococo pieces, such as carved furniture from Gillow & Co. of Lancaster and Henri Dasson of Paris and porcelain produced by Meissen from eighteenth-century molds or by Coalbrookdale in the manner of eighteenth-century Meissen and Sèvres.

The style reached its peak of fashion during the mid-VICTORIAN and early SECOND EMPIRE periods, epitomized by the many products directly imitative or broadly interpretive of the eighteenth-century idiom shown at the Crystal

Palace Exhibition in London in 1851, the New York Crystal Palace Exhibition in 1853–54, and at the Exposition Universelle in Paris in 1855. The style promulgated commercially was a heightened and more generalized Rococo—brighter, more insistently naturalistic, less linear, more sinuous and bulging, and more ample—including balloon-back chairs and deeply upholstered sofas with natural (not painted and gilded) wood, carpets emblazoned with large floral and architectural patterns, porcelain copiously decorated with applied flowers, and metalwork with scrollwork and vegetal ornamentation.

The vogue for Rococo Revival lasted longest in Germany, and it also had a distinctive, independent expression in the United States. This centered on the elaborately carved parlor suites by the German immigrant cabinetmaker John Henry Belter and his imitators. Using his own patented techniques, Belter manufactured molded, laminated rosewood furniture with exaggerated shapes and openwork designs of fruits, flowers, and foliage, which met with such widespread success that his work has become synonymous with the Rococo Revival in America.

RUGS—*see* CARPETS

SCHOOL OF FONTAINEBLEAU—*see* FRANCIS I

SECESSION

▷ **WHO** ARCHITECTS, ARTISTS, AND DESIGNERS: Josef Hoffmann, Gustav Klimt, Koloman Moser, Joseph Maria Olbrich, Otto Wagner
CRAFTSMEN AND MANUFACTURERS: Johann Backhausen & Söhne, Jacob & Josef Kohn, J. & L. Lobmeyr, Gebrüder Thonet, Wiener Werkstätte

▷ **WHEN** 1897 through 1910s

▷ **WHERE** Austria

▷ **WHAT** An Austrian variant of ART NOUVEAU, the Secession style took its name from the breakaway exhibition society founded in Vienna in 1897 by Josef Hoffmann, Koloman Moser, Joseph Maria Olbrich, and Gustav Klimt. It was popularized by the Secession magazine *Ver Sacrum* (Sacred Spring), published between 1898 and 1903, and by the Wiener Werkstätte (Vienna Workshop)—a crafts workshop and retail operation established in 1903 by Hoffmann and Moser (with Fritz Wärndorfer as a financial backer) to

JOSEF HOFFMANN (1870–1956).
Furnishing Fabric, 1902. Austrian. Linen and cotton, each repeat
15¹/₂ x 14³/₄ in. (39.5 x 37.5 cm). Würtembergisches Landesmuseum,
Stuttgart, Germany.

produce and market their designs and those by other artists. Inspired by the ARTS AND CRAFTS MOVEMENT, the Secession sought to lower the barriers between the fine and applied arts. Their exhibitions included not only paintings and sculpture but also interiors and furnishings by both Viennese and foreign, particularly British, artists—C. R. Ashbee and Charles Rennie Mackintosh among them. Like other reformers of the period, the Secession members sought stylistic unity and shared the ideal of the interior as a total work of art, with architecture, furnishings, and fine arts completely coordinated. Their earliest designs reflected the naturalistic, curvilinear forms and sinuous patterns of Art Nouveau (albeit more sober and static), but under the influence of Hoffmann and Moser the Secession developed its distinctive vocabulary of simple geometric shapes and ornaments; a palette of white, black, and gray; and compositions that were rectilinear, symmetrical, and repetitive.

This new style was given its most characteristic expression in the furniture, metalwork, jewelry, ceramics, glass, bookbinding, clothing, and graphics produced by the Werkstätte, which maintained a rigorous formalism with remarkable homogeneity. Chairs were constructed as geometrical patterns (squares, rectangles, and circles in repetition and combination); small wares made of enameled metal were pierced with a repetitive pattern of small square holes; and posters featured letterforms reduced to or squeezed into rectangles and bracketed with black-and-white rectangular patterns. Several buildings by Hoffmann were executed as total works of art, with furnishings supplied by the Wiener Werkstätte and a number of collaborating artists: the Pukersdorf Sanatorium (1904–6), the Palais Stoclet in Brussels (1905–11), and the Viennese cabaret Die Fledermaus (1907). For the Palais Stoclet, Klimt designed the mosaic frieze in the dining room (executed by Leopold Forstner); Carl Otto Czeschka, the windows for the theater and music room; Michael Powolny, a ceramic sculpture over the entrance; and Bertold Löffler, several small mosaic panels. Without abandoning the geometric aesthetic that made it a forerunner of MODERNISM, the Secession style became increasingly decorative and opulent—as in the colored marble panels; mosaics of marble, glass, and semiprecious stones; gilded metalwork; and patterned and pictorial colored tiles in the Palais Stoclet and Fledermaus interiors.

SECOND EMPIRE

▷ **WHO** ARCHITECTS AND DESIGNERS: Jules Pierre-Michel Diéterle CRAFTSMEN AND MANUFACTURERS: Thomas-Joseph Armand-Calliat, Léon Arnoux, Charles-Jean Avisseau, Ferdinand Barbedienne, Alfred Beurdeley,

Joseph Brocard, Charles Christofle, Cristalleries de Baccarat, Cristalleries de Saint-Louis, Michel-Victor Cruchet, Joseph-Théodore Deck, Jules Desfossé, Charles-Guillaume Diehl, Fannière Frères, Alexandre-Georges Fourdinois, Henri-Auguste Fourdinois, P.-H. Emile Froment-Meurice, Gibus et Cie, Gobelins tapestry factory, Guillaume Grohé, Haviland & Co., Charles-Joseph-Marie Jeanselme, Joseph-Pierre-François Jeanselme, Lamy et Giraud, Jean-Valentin Morel, Léonard Morel-Ladeuil, Claudius Popelin, Placide Poussielgue-Rusand, Sèvres porcelain factory, Marc-Louis-Emanuel Solon, Antoine Vechte

▷ **WHEN** 1852 to 1870

▷ **WHERE** France

▷ **WHAT** *Second Empire* encompasses the various styles current in France during the reign of Louis-Napoleon Bonaparte as Emperor Napoleon III (1852–70). The taste for historic revival (*see* RENAISSANCE REVIVAL, ROCOCO REVIVAL) that had developed under LOUIS-PHILIPPE reached its height of popularity during the Second Empire, when Paris fashions were followed from Moscow to New York. With increasing freedom and virtuosity, designers borrowed the forms of past styles, mixed them eclectically, and interpreted them in modern materials. Mechanization facilitated the spread and variety of styles, lowering prices and encouraging novelties. Elaborate detail, decoration, color, and ornament were used, whatever the style, to achieve the effects of richness universally admired during the period. In interior design, fashion dictated certain styles for certain uses: drawing rooms were LOUIS XV or LOUIS XVI, with gilded wood and damask upholstery; dining rooms were RENAISSANCE, with carved paneling and a monumental buffet; the bedroom suite was Louis XVI, with delicate gilded furniture and a skirted dressing table, following Empress Eugénie's passion for the style of Marie Antoinette. These interiors were modernized by the addition of comfortable, upholstered, tufted chairs and ottomans—introduced in the 1820s and 1830s but not widely adopted until the Second Empire. While great houses paraded a variety of historic styles, certain critics, Prosper Mérimée among them, criticized such studied eclecticism as evidence of a lack of originality and purpose.

A new and unusually colorful form of NEOCLASSICISM called Néo-Grec, invented in the 1840s, became popular, with original combinations of eclectic forms and motifs from Egyptian, Etruscan, Greek, and Roman sources. The so-called Pompeian House in Paris, built and decorated in 1860 for Prince Napoleon, cousin of the emperor, was an influential example. Exotic styles from the Near and Far East were also adopted, Japanese art being of particular consequence following the opening of Japan to the West by the American Commodore Matthew Perry in 1852 and the Japanese display at the International Exhibition of 1862 in London (see AESTHETIC MOVEMENT). The great international exhibitions held in London in 1851 and 1862 and in Paris in 1855 and 1867 provided arenas where French manufacturers competed with English and other foreign firms for markets and prestige. A number of French designers found work in England, spreading the Second Empire style abroad during the VICTORIAN era. Among them were Léon Arnoux and Marc-Louis-Emanuel Solon, who both worked for the Minton porcelain factory, and Antoine Vechte and Léonard Morel-Ladeuil, who both worked for Elkington, the electroplate manufacturers.

SHAKER

Forsaking fashion, style, and originality for conformity to models established by their spiritual leaders, the American Shaker sect produced simple, unornamented, superbly crafted objects that met virtually every need of their utopian, communal life. From modest beginnings in the late eighteenth century, the United Society of Believers—or Shakers, as they were called after the defining form of their dance worship—grew by about 1850 to comprise some twenty communities in the East and Midwest, populated by several thousand members. Celibate, the Shakers lived in planned villages grouped into smaller units called Families, and were housed in neat structures built and furnished with the fruits of their own labor. The care they devoted to all aspects of their life was a product of the belief that outward appearances should reflect the harmony of the inner spirit.

Shaker craftsmen uniformly took as their models the plain COUNTRY furniture of the FEDERAL period. Although the forms of their work were repetitive, the repeated subtle variations in construction and execution permit the attribution of pieces to specific communities. Chests, tables, workstands, pegboards (used throughout their buildings), built-in cupboards, and light, turned chairs and rockers were individualized to fit the particular use each piece would have. Fashioned of pine, maple, or fruit and nut woods, the furniture was generally varnished or painted in one or two solid, saturated colors. (The paint was often stripped off earlier in this century by collectors who found the spare practicality of Shaker design in natural wood well suited to the aesthetics of MODERNISM, and even by surviving Shakers themselves.)

Spool Box, c. 1825–40. Made in Canterbury, New Hampshire. Maple, pine, chestnut, copper tacks, and silk and cotton thread, 3¹/₄ x 9¹/₂ x 6³/₄ in. (8.2 x 24.1 x 17.1 cm). Philadelphia Museum of Art; Gift of Mr. and Mrs. Julius Zieget.

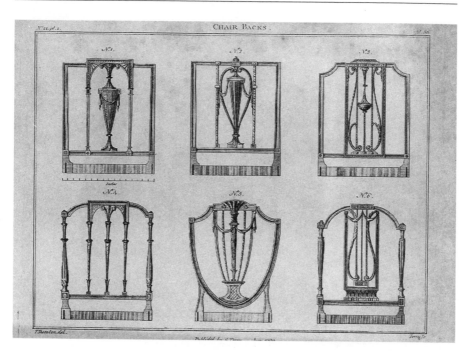

Plate 36 from Thomas Sheraton "The Cabinet-Maker and Upholsterer's Drawing Book," London, 1791–94. The Metropolitan Museum of Art Library, New York.

From the 1850s the Mount Lebanon, New York, community developed a thriving chair industry (it lasted until the 1930s), which supplied other communities as well as the outside world with a line of slat-backed chairs upholstered in plush or with woven fabric tapes, with or without arms and rockers. These were sold in retail outlets and through illustrated catalogs, the first issued in 1874. Other notable Shaker manufactures included oval, molded-splint boxes; BASKETRY; a wide range of inventive tools; woolen capes (made in Canterbury, New Hampshire, from about 1890 to 1940), and printed ephemera connected with the Shaker seed and herb industry. In the mid-nineteenth century, during a period of spiritual revival, a number of Shakers created "gift" drawings, designs in watercolor said to represent divine visions.

SHERATON

▷ **WHO** Thomas Sheraton

▷ **WHEN** 1790s to early 1800s

▷ **WHERE** England

▷ **WHAT** The Sheraton style is based on the plates in Thomas Sheraton's furniture pattern books, principally his *Cabinet-Maker and Upholsterer's Drawing-Book*, which were published periodically between 1791 and 1794. This style of furniture draws together many elements of late-eighteenth-century English NEOCLASSICISM, but it is both more refined and more severe, with rectilinear outlines, delicate flat (rather than carved) decoration, and coloristic effects achieved with paint or inlays of various woods.

A teacher of "Perspective, Architecture and Ornaments," according to his trade card, as well as a creator of "Designs for Cabinet-makers," Sheraton is not known to have made any furniture himself, and there are few pieces by other craftsmen that replicate his plates directly. Following George HEPPLE-WHITE'S *Cabinet-Maker and Upholsterer's Guide* (1788) by only a few years and wedged between the ADAM style of the eighteenth century and the REGENCY style of the early nineteenth (to which it contributed), Sheraton's book documented the advanced trends of his time but invented relatively little. The most characteristic new features are those of his typical side chairs: plain tapered legs, a square seat, and a square open back with vertical bars that support antique decorative motifs.

Whereas Sheraton's *Drawing-Book* adopted Adam's type of freely inspired ornament after the antique, his *Cabinet-Maker, Upholsterer, and General Artist's Encyclopaedia* (1804–6) was among the first pattern books to include designs that borrowed specifically from antique prototypes, such as ancient animal motifs and the curved-back, saber-legged *klismos* chair. Sheraton's designs were very influential in the United States during the FEDERAL period, becoming known either directly from his books or through the interpretations of intermediary American craftsmen's publications. The New York cabinetmaker Duncan Phyfe relied heavily on Sheraton's work.

SILVER—*see* GOLD AND SILVER

STATUETTES

Statuettes are freestanding, small-scale figures or figure groups made in boxwood, bronze, gold and silver, ivory, porcelain, pottery, wax, or other materials. Bronze statuettes were used in antiquity as votive offerings and private devotional objects (such as the lares, or Roman household gods). During the RENAISSANCE, aristocrats collected small classical bronzes and displayed them side by side with works by contemporary sculptors, such as Antico, one of a number of Renaissance artists who made small bronze reductions of the most famous pieces of ancient sculpture. Commercial adaptations or variants of these works in stucco and terra-cotta were also sold by large workshops. The taste for small original and reproduction bronzes lasted well into the twentieth century, catered to finally by ART NOUVEAU and ART DECO sculptors such as Demêtre Chiparus, who combined painted bronze with ivory to achieve naturalistic effects.

During the seventeenth century, when Chinese porcelains began to arrive in Europe in quantity, the fashion for using porcelain statuettes and vessels in interior decoration developed in court circles. It was introduced in England at Hampton Court Palace, where porcelains were often arranged on stepped ledges above the corner chimneypieces and later, according to the novelist Daniel Defoe, piled on cabinets, desks, and shelves. As the European porcelain industries developed during the eighteenth century, porcelain statuettes were widely used as ornaments at grand dessert tables, replacing figures made of wax or confectionery. These porcelains were often designed by sculptors in large series that also included miniature temples and garden furniture of potted trees, fountains, and urns, which could all be assembled on a mirror plateau, or stand. More often, however, statuettes in porcelain

VAN DER VOORST (n.d.) after François Boucher (1703–1770).
The Jealous Suitor, c. 1756. Made by the Sèvres porcelain factory.
Biscuit porcelain, height: 9½ in. (24 cm). Musée des Arts Décoratifs,
Paris.

or less expensive pottery were made in complementary pairs or in sets such as the Four Seasons, some with branches and holders for candles. These were displayed on mantels or on "china" tables or shelves, as indicated in Thomas CHIPPENDALE's *Gentleman and Cabinet-Maker's Director* (1754). This fashion had largely waned among the wealthy by the end of the eighteenth century, but during the nineteenth century a large commercial industry in pottery statuettes developed in Staffordshire, England, for a middle-class VICTORIAN market. Its production included a wide range of subjects in naive styles, from figures of Queen Victoria and Prince Albert to poodles and other animals. Similar products were made in America at the Bennington, Vermont, pottery factory.

STILE LIBERTY—*see* ART NOUVEAU

STUART—*see* JACOBEAN, RESTORATION, WILLIAM AND MARY

TAPESTRIES

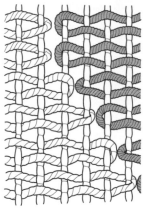

TAPESTRY WEAVE

Tapestry is a technique of pictorial or ornamental weaving in which the design is created as part of the structure of the fabric. The colored wefts are carried on bobbins and woven across the warp threads in distinct colored areas—not across the entire piece, as in the manufacture of other textiles. Where two colors meet, a longitudinal slit occurs. Since this tends to weaken the fabric, several techniques are used to avoid slits and blend the colors: dovetailing, or alternating, colored yarns in comb and sawtooth forms; hatching, a broader form of dovetailing that creates long spikes of adjacent colors; and looping or interlocking the yarns. These features and the creation of curves with staggers or steps, along with the characteristic ribbed surface, give tapestries their distinctive appearance.

Tapestries are woven on simple looms, a frame with a roller on each end, with the warps wound around one roller and taken up on the other as the weaving proceeds. Two forms of looms were used by European tapestry factories, each giving equally fine results: low-warp *(basse-lisse* in French) looms, resembling standard shuttle looms in which the warp threads are horizontal; and high-warp *(haute-lisse),* or upright looms, in which the warp threads are vertical. In the high-warp technique, the weaver sat behind the loom, viewing the front of the tapestry in a mirror; the cartoon, or full-size drawing, was behind the weaver, who could compare it in the mirror with the tapestry in process.

During the Middle Ages, tapestries were used as wall hangings, table covers, bed canopies and coverings, and cushions. Northern France and Flanders (particularly Brussels, Tournai, Poitiers, and Arras, which gave its name to tapestry hangings) were the centers of large-scale tapestry weaving; smaller workshops were plentiful in Germany and Switzerland. Subjects included biblical and historical themes, armorial designs, allegories, *verdures* (landscapes abundant with foliage and wildlife), and *millefleurs,* with hundreds of flowers dotting the surface, used most famously in the Unicorn tapestries, woven about 1490–1500 (Musée Nationale de Moyen Age, Paris).

Such late Gothic flat patterning was left behind as Italian RENAISSANCE painting made its mark, notably with the weaving of the Acts of the Apostles, a series of ten tapestries based on cartoons by Raphael and ordered from the weaver Peter van Aelst of Brussels by Pope Leo X in 1515 for the Sistine Chapel. These proved so successful that they were woven again and again, in Brussels and elsewhere, including by the JACOBEAN workshop at Mortlake in London (with borders designed by Peter Paul Rubens) and at Gobelins in Paris. Many other important Renaissance and BAROQUE artists, such as Giulio Romano, Rubens, Bernard Van Orley, and David Teniers, created cartoons for tapestries that became, in effect, woven paintings.

Tapestries became a currency of royalty, and royal workshops were opened throughout Europe: by Gustav I of Sweden (1523), FRANCIS I of France (at Fontainebleau in the 1530s), Phillip II of Spain (1579), Frederick II of Denmark (at Elsinore from 1581), Henri IV of France (at two Paris workshops, in 1589 and 1607), Elector Maximilian of Bavaria (in Munich in 1604), James I of England (at Mortlake in 1619), LOUIS XIV (at Gobelins in 1662), and Peter the Great (in Saint Petersburg in 1716).

During the eighteenth century, tapestry production was led by French workshops, notably Beauvais, which had great success with ROCOCO designs by its director Jean-Baptiste Oudry and by François Boucher, including his *Fêtes italiennes* (begun in 1736) and *Tentures chinoises (Chinese Hangings)* (begun in 1743). Instead of being set in floral and scrollwork borders, scenes were now placed within woven gilded frames that simulated interior woodwork.

Tapestries, also used for UPHOLSTERY, were part of new interior conceptions, intermingling figurative or decorative subjects with ornamental elements such as architectural fragments and canopies, arabesques, statuary, scroll-work, trophies, and garlands. This style is typified by the grotesques after Jean Berain woven at Beauvais between about 1690 and 1710; the arabesques woven at Soho in London about 1720; and the *alentours* (surroundings) tapestries woven at Gobelins early in the eighteenth century. The last named had "framed" pictures after designs by Boucher, Charles-Antoine Coypel, and others hung against walls of damask surrounded with moldings and strung with trompe l'oeil floral garlands, animals, and other naturalistic elements, which were the work of other designers.

Tapestry declined in the nineteenth century as industrial production replaced craft industries. Toward the end of the century, however, two important workshops revived the craft in England. One, at Windsor, founded by Queen Victoria and in operation from 1876 to 1890, supplied the royal households with high-quality series with historical and literary subjects. The other, established by William Morris at Merton Abbey in 1881, produced weavings after medieval-inspired designs by Morris, Edward Burne-Jones, Walter Crane, and others in the ARTS AND CRAFTS MOVEMENT. The craft of tapestry weaving was brought to America around the turn of the century by two workshops in New York, both employing French weavers, those of William Baumgarten and Albert Herter, working, respectively, in ROCOCO REVIVAL and Morris-inspired Gothic styles. The weaving of tapestries in Scandinavia, a traditional women's FOLK ART since the seventeenth century, was also revived at this time—notably, in Norway with the encouragement of the Norwegian Weaving Society.

TEXTILES—*see* UPHOLSTERY

TILES

Tiles are flat slabs of fired clay in square, rectangular, lozenge, and other shapes, used to cover floors, pavements, and walls. Used in large numbers, they can be conceived either as individual elements; in multiples, in which certain design motifs are completed only when joined in four or more units; or as elements of a pictorial composition. Like other forms of POTTERY, tiles may be coated with lead and tin glazes and embellished with inlaid (encaustic), incised, impressed, or monochrome and polychrome painted decoration. Redware floor tiles, plain or with contrasting slip decoration, were used

Tiles: Animals in Scalloped Roundels, 1625–50. Dutch. Glazed ceramic, each approximately 5¼ x 5¼ in. (13.4 x 13.4 cm). Philadelphia Museum of Art; Gift of Edward W. Bok.

in Europe in ecclesiastical and other important buildings during the Middle Ages; they were reintroduced in the nineteenth century, especially in England in GOTHIC REVIVAL churches and in interiors associated with the ARTS AND CRAFTS MOVEMENT. Wall tiles in the Moorish style were used in Spain from the fifteenth century. They were made with two different techniques devised to keep the colors from running together during firing: *cuerda seca,* in which designs were outlined with a greasy substance to repel the glazes; and *cuenca,* in which impressed geometric designs were filled with pools of glaze that became luminescent upon firing.

Tin-glazed, or majolica, tiles with colored designs painted on white ground were first made by Italian potteries in the late fifteenth century; these hexagonal tiles, used for floors, had ornamental patterns and figural subjects, such as portraits in roundels. Italian potters took the majolica technique to Antwerp in the sixteenth century, and craftsmen in the Low Countries quickly adapted it to the production of tiles, soon made in standard five-inch squares, which were used primarily for walls and fireplace surrounds. Merging two traditions, majolica decoration and the earlier monochrome floor tiles, they created in single and four-tile units polychrome designs of fruits, flowers, animals, and other subjects. These were alternated with blue ornaments in reserve (i.e., the background was painted to define the design), which evolved over the next century into the minuscule corner motifs that give later Dutch tile panels their repeating and unifying motifs.

By 1625, with the increasing popularity of imported Chinese blue-and-white porcelains, polychrome decoration had been mainly replaced with monochrome, most often in blue. Made in Delft and elsewhere in the Netherlands, these tiles were exported and copied throughout Europe and used on notable buildings from France (the Trianon de Porcelaine built by LOUIS XIV at Versailles, 1670–87) to Poland (the grand staircase of the palace of Nieborów, c. 1765). Delft tiles included a wide range of subjects (biblical scenes, children's games, tradesmen, animals, ships, and soldiers), many derived from engraved sources; they were also made as pictures from multiple tiles, mainly blue, manganese, and polychrome floral and still-life subjects.

Nineteenth-century wall tiles frequently depended on revival styles, including the Persian designs by William De Morgan in England and the medieval and historical subjects used by Henry Chapman Mercer at his Doylestown, Pennsylvania, works. Other companies followed contemporary styles, such as the encaustic AESTHETIC MOVEMENT tiles influenced by Japanese motifs made by the Low Art Tile Works of Chelsea, Massachusetts.

TIN

Tin is a bluish-white metal that is unusually malleable but not ductile (able to be drawn into thin wires without breaking). It is very soft, bends readily, and can be hammered or pressed into thin sheets, such as tinfoil. Tin resists corrosion and is often used as a coating for other metals, including COPPER, IRON, and steel. Known since antiquity, tin has been used more in alloys than in its pure form because of its softness. However, certain utensils and ornamental products—jewelry in the ancient world, masks and other FOLK ART objects produced today in Mexico—are made of tin, valued for the color and luster of the metal and for the ease with which it can be worked. Tin-plated sheet iron, known as "tole," was developed in England in the late seventeenth century and produced in Europe and America during the eighteenth and nineteenth centuries—most commonly in the form of small useful wares such as canisters and trays with LACQUER decorations.

TOYS AND GAMES

Not until the eighteenth century did craftsmen begin to specialize in the making of toys and games, starting in Germany, where firms such as that of Gottfried Hilpert made tin soldiers, animals, and circus figures based on actual models. Earlier (and still), craftsmen and artists would create toys and games in addition to their usual products—from the country carpenter who constructed a wagon or a rocking horse out of scrap wood to the German RENAISSANCE clockmakers who fabricated mechanical toys (or "automata") and the ART NOUVEAU designers who created chess pieces out of glass and ceramics. Although made in great numbers, relatively few toys and games survive because of hard use and the nature of their materials. Dolls, for example, are generally fashioned in combinations of fabric, wax, wood, porcelain, pottery, paper, papier-mâché, and celluloid and other plastics, which makes them vulnerable to light, heat, moisture, abrasion, and insects. Some, such as French bisque fashion dolls, notably those made by Jumeau in Paris between 1842 and 1899 (which could be dressed with a trunkful of the latest styles), were prized and passed down as heirlooms, but most dolls show signs of extreme wear.

MAX ESSER (1885–1943).
Chessmen and Chessboard, 1925. Made by the Meissen porcelain
factory, Meissen, Germany. Hard-paste porcelain, height of king:
3¼ in. (8.3 cm). Philadelphia Museum of Art; Gift of John F. Harbeson.

Many toys are miniature reproductions of figures, animals, buildings, and utilitarian objects, often minutely and realistically detailed. (These should be distinguished, however, from small craftsmen's models, which were made for commercial purposes.) Some miniatures are so meticulously done that they reflect clearly the specific styles and periods of their manufacture. Among these are architectural replicas, such as the dollhouses with a complete array of living and service quarters that became popular in Europe during the seventeenth and eighteenth centuries (for example, the eighteenth-century English dollhouse from Nostell Priory in Yorkshire, England, attributed to Thomas CHIPPENDALE, with its opulent Neoclassical drawing room). Complete armies of soldiers—like the 1914 Allied forces of French, Belgian, Russian, and British infantry with distinctive uniforms and equipment produced by the Parisian firm of C. B. G. Mignot—and trains, such as the Vaucalin compound engine, tender, and other cars modeled on the rolling stock that ran on the New York Central Railroad around the turn of the century, were also made with a high degree of authentic detail.

Games played with dice, markers, and counters and game boards have been popular since ancient times. Chess, which was brought to Europe from India and Persia, was well established among the noble classes by the early Middle Ages. Chess pieces, in stylized shapes taking the form of feudal figures in battle, evolved from Indian imagery of elephants and royal personages and were made of crystal, amber, horn, ivory, or silver. Over time, chess sets have been modeled on many different themes, from John Flaxman's figures from Shakespeare designed for Wedgwood in 1783 and Indian EXPORT WARES depicting the British and the Hindus to modernist geometric shapes made by Joseph Hartwig at the Bauhaus in 1924. In the nineteenth century, French, English, and German manufacturers made chess sets based on actual wars and battles, both historical and contemporary, including the defeat of the Spanish Armada, the Battle of Waterloo, the Crimean War, and the Franco-Prussian War.

TUDOR

▷ **WHO** ARTIST: Hans Holbein
CRAFTSMEN AND MANUFACTURERS: Thomas Geminus, Nicholas Hilliard, Richard Hyckes, William Sheldon, Jacopo Verzelini

▷ **WHEN** 1485 to 1603

▷ **WHERE** England

▷ **WHAT** During the reign of the Tudor monarchs (1485–1603), an age of greatly expanding wealth and power, elements of the RENAISSANCE style began to appear in England, where rich classical ornamentation from Italy mingled with the remnants of late-medieval forms and native craftsmanship. Renaissance influence came with the foreign artists and craftsmen patronized by Henry VIII (reigned 1509–47), and later through the mannered Flemish and German interpretations in the engravings and pattern books imported during the reign of his daughter Elizabeth I (1558–1603). Classical motifs—such as cherubs, portrait heads in roundels, acanthus leaves, and arabesques of fruits, flowers, and other natural forms—spread throughout the arts in England, mainly as surface decoration. They appeared on the facades of the stone and brick country houses that the nobility began to build at the end of the sixteenth century; on the new paneled (or wainscotted) rooms as well as their plasterwork ceilings and chimneypieces; on magnificent silver-gilt saltcellars and other table ornaments; and on voluminous needlework hangings for beds.

Furniture, primarily of oak, was massive, rectilinear, and heavily carved: great four-poster beds; box chairs with carved backs and turned legs (used by the master of the house); jointed stools (the seating for others); paneled cupboards and chests, some inlaid with conventionalized naturalistic ornament or architectural views; plank trestle tables; and "drawing" tables, which doubled in length when the leaves were drawn out at the ends. By the Elizabethan era, large, bulbous forms turned and carved with foliage and gadrooning following the shape and ornamentation of silver cups and covers had become characteristic for table legs, bed posts, and supports on court (short) cupboards with open shelves.

Ceremonial table silver was grand in scale, decorated with mythological figures and a profusion of grotesques, much of it influenced by the designs of Hans Holbein (who created jewelry, court costumes, and festival decorations for the court of Henry VIII) and other foreign artists. Similarly elaborate mounts in silver were added to prized exotic imports, such as porcelain from China, ostrich eggs, coconuts, coral, and hardstones. Table implements were rudimentary; silver or pewter spoons, most commonly with pear-shaped bowls and circular or polygonal handles, were the principal eating implements until the fork came into wide use during the RESTORATION. Small industries produced engraved Venetian-style soda GLASS (manufactured after 1574 by the Italian Jacopo Verzelini) and tapestries (at William Sheldon's factory founded after 1560), crafts that would become significant in the JACOBEAN period.

Cup, 1567. English. Oriental agate and silver gilt, height: 7³/₄ in. (19.7 cm). Victoria and Albert Museum, London.

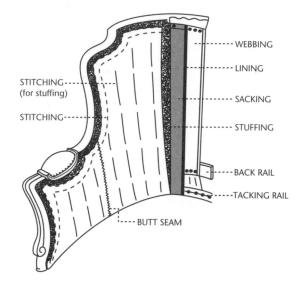

STITCHING
(for stuffing)

STITCHING

WEBBING

LINING

SACKING

STUFFING

BACK RAIL

TACKING RAIL

BUTT SEAM

BACK OF CHAIR

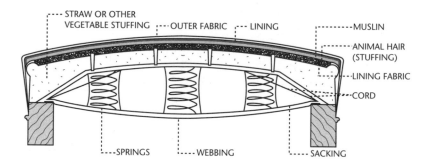

STRAW OR OTHER
VEGETABLE STUFFING

OUTER FABRIC

LINING

MUSLIN

ANIMAL HAIR
(STUFFING)

LINING FABRIC

CORD

SPRINGS

WEBBING

SACKING

CROSS SECTION—CHAIR SEAT

UPHOLSTERY

Traditionally, *upholstery* referred to the varied textiles used to furnish interiors, whether as wall or door hangings, window curtains, carpets, or coverings and cushions for furniture. Today, upholstery is more narrowly defined as textile furnishings for seating. The upholsterer's craft developed rapidly in seventeenth-century Europe as living standards and notions of comfort rose. Unless a BAROQUE room was paneled, it usually had wall hangings that ranged from simple woolen or worsted materials to richly figured silk damasks or gilt leather (the latter was particularly popular in Holland, Germany, and Scandinavia). Except for gilt leather, the same materials were used for bed hangings, which were heavy and lined for warmth. Window curtains were usually of thinner fabrics, like silk taffeta. Chairs were simple in form, with rectangular seats and backs covered by fabrics fixed with nails. The seats were made comfortable with fillings of vegetable fiber, wool, or hair, supported by webbing and covered with linen cloth; these under-upholsteries were covered in any number of materials, such as Turkey work (see NEEDLEWORK), tapestry, leather, embroidered silk, or the crimson silk velvet finished with fringe that decorates the celebrated and still-surviving couch at Knole in Kent, England.

By the early eighteenth century, window curtains began to be treated more decoratively, with pelmets (valances) masking the curtain heads and a new system of pulleys and cords to draw the curtains into elegant swags or festoons. The craft of upholstering furniture also developed rapidly, using techniques borrowed from saddlemakers to arrange the stuffing more evenly over seats and keep it in position by padding and stitching the edges. Cushions, or "squabs," as they were called in England, continued to be used on stools, chairs, and daybeds, all of which, particularly in England and Holland, were often caned. The cushions were squared and tufted like mattresses to keep the stuffing in place, then tied to the seat and back with tapes or ribbons. Among new forms of upholstered furniture were sofas and armchairs with deep, down-filled cushions lying in a well in the seat and with backs padded with springy horsehair. Instead of heavy braids and fringes, the edges of the furniture were finished with closely spaced rows of nails, sometimes in decorative patterns. The rich coverings on such upholstered furniture usually related to or matched the hangings on walls, beds, and windows, and were detachable or protected by loose covers when not in use.

By the mid-eighteenth century, ROCOCO coverings also included exotic imported fabrics, such as painted Chinese silk taffetas or Indian painted cottons, used particularly in country houses. Curtain materials continued to be lightweight. While single-festoon curtains were common all over Europe, in England and America curtains that were divided in half and pulled up diagonally toward the outer corners of the window were also popular. In the 1790s festoons became purely decorative and were also used on NEOCLASSICAL furniture. They were attached between the legs and across the backs of seats, used on beds, and draped decoratively over curtain poles, while secondary curtains or roller blinds did the work of excluding light from windows.

Upholsterers experimented with different ways of stuffing, including forms of springing, but it was not until the mid-nineteenth century that the metal coil spring was produced in quantity. Larger and deeper seats were required to accommodate the use of large numbers of springs. Springing, used in connection with the deeply buttoned upholsteries so popular in VICTORIAN and SECOND EMPIRE furniture, was facilitated by new button-making and buttoning machines. Two other machines assisted the upholsterer at the turn of the century: the carding machine, which aided the production of worsted materials, and the sewing machine. In nineteenth-century interiors, heavy outer curtains of silk or worsted damask were typically combined with inner curtains of muslin or lace. In the twentieth century, furniture became increasingly machine-made; upholsteries became simpler, selected for maintenance, wearability, and economy rather than showy appearance. Leather, cane, and canvas used with tubular-steel furniture in the 1920s, for example (see MODERNISM), were considered cleaner and more modern materials than a fabric like velvet, which was said to "hold dust," although plush fabrics were favored by ART DECO designers. Modernist textile designers also embraced new man-made fibers, like cellophane, which were used to construct the light, open-weave curtains favored by progressives during the period.

VICTORIAN

▷ **WHO** ARCHITECTS, ARTISTS, AND DESIGNERS: Charles Barry, John Bell, Edward Burne-Jones, William Butterfield, Charles Locke Eastlake, Owen Jones, Edwin Landseer, Frederic Leighton, Joseph Paxton, A. W. N. Pugin, Richard Redgrave, John Rogers, George Gilbert Scott, Gottfried Semper, Alfred Stevens
CRAFTSMEN AND MANUFACTURERS: John Henry Belter, Coalport porcelain factory, John Gregory Crace, G. R. Elkington, R. & S. Garrard, Gillow & Co., Herter Brothers, Holland & Sons, Hunt & Roskell, Jennens & Bettridge, Minton & Co., Morris and Co., Rockingham porcelain factory
THEORISTS: Henry Cole, John Ruskin

▷ **WHEN** 1837 to 1901

▷ **WHERE** Great Britain and the United States

▷ **WHAT** Strictly speaking, the term *Victorian* should describe only work created in Great Britain and its vast empire during the long reign of Queen Victoria (1837–1901), an era noted for both its serious moral tone and its wanton materialism. In practice, however, the term encompasses the United States as well and is applied to objects made from the second quarter of the nineteenth century through the reign of Victoria's son Edward VII (1901–10) that exhibit an eclecticism of style and a delight in decoration, from an English Rockingham china vase blanketed with applied floral decoration to the wooden gingerbread scrollwork on a house in San Francisco. The style appealed to a large, newly affluent public who eagerly acquired artistic furnishings made by the latest techniques of industry, favored didactic art with sentimental and elevating subjects, and delighted in the comfort of sofas and chairs with capacious curves and deeply tufted UPHOLSTERY. They lived in rooms hung with voluminous draperies layered with braids, fringes, and tassels; sat in chairs upholstered with Berlin woolwork (see NEEDLEWORK); and walked on machine-woven Ingrain CARPETS from Kidderminster and pile carpets with large patterns of flowers, scrollwork, and architectural elements.

Like the LOUIS-PHILIPPE and SECOND EMPIRE styles in France, Victorian was not one style but many, all sharing a rich ornamentalism and a dependence on historical models. These were approached with some concern for antiquarian accuracy early in the period and with considerably more independence later on, many aspects of the styles having already become hopelessly intertwined by midcentury: antique revivals (see NEOCLASSICISM), period revivals (see GOTHIC REVIVAL, RENAISSANCE REVIVAL, ROCOCO REVIVAL), an extremely realistic depiction of nature, and exotic expressions from all over the globe (many derived from the patterns in Owen Jones's *Grammar of Ornament*, 1856). One of these styles, however, has come to be identified popularly as Victorian—the Rococo Revival, in its most mixed and eclectic form. It drew heavily on the LOUIS XV style, combining opulent and exaggerated ROCOCO forms with luxuriant naturalistic decoration. The Rococo Revival reached its height in England by the 1850s but remained popular in the United States for several decades after that, owing much of its success to the elaborately carved rosewood furniture sold by the New York firm of John Henry Belter and its imitators.

Aspects of Victorian self-criticism were manifest in the emergence of antihistorical, reform styles, which promoted simplicity and honesty in the use of materials and workmanship (see AESTHETIC MOVEMENT, ARTS AND CRAFTS MOVE-MENT), although these are sometimes distanced from the period's psyche by today's critics and reckoned as forerunners of MODERNISM. Early in the century, the unbridled production of manufactured goods, including many made of cheap materials, had brought calls for new standards of taste and design in Britain. The improvement of design through the employment of artists as designers for industry was advocated by Henry Cole and Richard Redgrave in the *Journal of Design* (1847–49). Industrial production was questioned by the critic John Ruskin, who rejected technology for the honest craftsmanship of the medieval period, and later by William Morris, who sought a renewal of English design in small communities of designers following the craft techniques of earlier periods (although it did not keep him from creating designs for machine-made carpets and textiles).

But the great Victorian achievement was its mastery of technology and mass production, showcased at the Crystal Palace Exhibition in London in 1851 and the series of international trade expositions that followed. They proudly featured new inventions, techniques, and materials—imaginative forms of lighting for oil and gas illumination; fine lace created by machine; cheap silver hollow ware made by Elkington's electroplating process (see GOLD AND SILVER); iron cast into garden furniture and brass made into beds; papier-mâché molded into decorative goods and furnishings; furniture made and decorated by numerous machine-carving processes—all the fruits of nineteenth-century industrialization and mercantilism.

WALLPAPER

Decorated wallpapers, known in Europe since the early sixteenth century, became widely used by the eighteenth, rivaling and then supplanting as wall coverings paneling, textiles, tapestries, and gilded leather, all of which wallpaper has often imitated. Floral designs and patterns resembling figured textiles—embroidery, velvets, damasks—and embossed leather were applied to rolls of paper, starting in the seventeenth century, by hand painting, woodblock printing, and such special techniques as flocking, in which powdered wool or silk is made to adhere to designs printed or stenciled in glue in order to create colored, textured patterns. Originally tacked, as well as pasted, to walls, wallpaper was also often mounted on stretched canvas, the form in which many antique papers, especially scenic sets, are also found today.

During the seventeenth and eighteenth centuries, Chinese painted scenic papers embellished with flowers, animals, and birds created a vogue in Europe for larger, colorful designs and exotic landscapes. This was echoed in

KATE GREENAWAY (1846–1901).
The Months, 1893. English. Made by David Walker and Co.
Machine-printed paper, 23½ x 22¼ in. (59.7 x 56.5 cm). The Whitworth
Art Gallery, University of Manchester, Manchester, England.

the printed CHINOISERIE papers produced in England and France, which were the centers of European wallpaper production during the eighteenth century. By the nineteenth century, papers simulating interior architectural components—dadoes, moldings, borders, friezes, latticework, and stuccowork, as well as columns and pilasters—were becoming popular, along with trompe l'oeil curtains and draperies. Most spectacular were the room-size sets of topographical views and scenes based on history, literature, and mythology, a specialty of French wallpaper firms. The suites produced by Jean Zuber and Joseph Dufour early in the century were printed with a restricted palette of flat, clear colors, but by the SECOND EMPIRE, Jules Desfossé was brilliantly printing designs with hundreds of blocks in a profusion of subtle tones meant to rival the art of painting.

Industrialization had made a strong mark by midcentury, particularly in England, and machine-printed papers, produced in great numbers, began to be sold side by side with hand-printed ones. Concurrently, British reformers, railing against the VICTORIAN use of extremely naturalistic motifs and a multiplicity of patterns, promoted designs that emphasized the flatness of the wall surface. This new approach was initiated in A. W. N. Pugin's heraldic GOTHIC REVIVAL papers for the Houses of Parliament in London (1836–37) and encouraged by the wealth of flat patterns published in the color plates of Owen Jones's influential *Grammar of Ornament* (1856). Later in the century it was reflected in the dense, stylized floral papers designed by William Morris and in papers by other artists of the ARTS AND CRAFTS MOVEMENT who followed Morris into pattern design, including Walter Crane and C. F. A. Voysey. Artist-designers of the ART NOUVEAU and ART DECO periods created original papers— among them, Hector Guimard, Henry van de Velde, Otto Eckmann, Emile-Jacques Ruhlmann, and Donald Deskey. Wallpaper patterns have had great longevity, remaining in pattern books over many decades, and numerous historical designs have periodically been revived and reproduced, especially in the early part of this century.

WIENER WERKSTÄTTE—*see* SECESSION

WILLIAM AND MARY

▷ **WHO** ARCHITECTS AND DESIGNERS: Daniel Marot, William Talman, Christopher Wren
CRAFTSMEN AND MANUFACTURERS: John Coney, George Garthorne, John Guilbaud, Pierre II Harache, Gerrit Jensen, Joseph Knibb, Francis Lapierre, James Morley, Jean Pelletier, Pierre Platel, Jean Tijou, Thomas Tompion

Bureau Cabinet, 1690–1700. English. Lacquered pine, silver gilt, and glass, 87 x 41 x 23³/4 in. (221 x 104.1 x 60.3 cm). The Collection of the Frick Art Museum, Pittsburgh.

▷ **WHEN** 1689 to 1702

▷ **WHERE** England and America

▷ **WHAT** During the short period that the Dutch prince William of Orange and his wife, Mary, ruled England as William (reigned 1689–1702) and Mary (reigned 1689–94), the BAROQUE style, now particularly French in form, continued to dominate production for the court. Its popularity was fueled by the arrival of numerous foreign craftsmen, especially large numbers of Huguenots fleeing France after the revocation of the Edict of Nantes in 1685. Most important economically were the thousands of Huguenot weavers from the silk centers of France, who settled east of London at Spitalfields and virtually transplanted the French silk industry to English soil, but Huguenot metalworkers also were significant and soon dominated the goldsmith and silversmith trades.

The Frenchman Daniel Marot, William's chief designer, who had worked at his court in Holland, was the foremost disseminator of the LOUIS XIV furnishing style in England, both through his work for the court (1694–98) and through his etched and engraved decorative designs. First published as a large collection of prints in 1703, his designs for vases, mirrors, clocks, candelabra, textiles, embroidery, upholstery, and furniture were meant to bring a unified style to decoration, as demonstrated in his designs for fully furnished interiors, such as bedchambers featuring great upholstered beds of state outfitted with elaborately constructed hangings and matching wall and furniture coverings. A similar French formality was introduced in the ironwork balconies, railings, and gates—most notably those for Hampton Court Palace—designed by the French ironsmith Jean Tijou and published in his *New Book of Drawings* (1693).

French influence is clearly evident in the court furniture with Boulle marquetries (see FURNITURE) after Marot's designs made by the cabinetmaker Gerrit Jensen; the sets of carved and gilded tables, mirrors, and candlestands by Jean Pelletier; and the equally Baroque silver furniture and carved stands for lacquer or japanned cabinets. With the economy and accessibility of Vauxhall glass, mirrors gained in popularity; they were used for bureau bookcases and toilet mirrors and stands, pier glasses placed between windows, and large overmantels, becoming significant new elements in interior decoration. A more rectilinear form of William and Mary furniture that drew on the Dutch sources that had been influential during the RESTORATION— particularly high chests of drawers, secretary cabinets, and fall-front desks with floral marquetry, burl walnut veneering, and japanned decoration, as well as high-back chairs with cane seats and backs—was also in vogue; these were the William and Mary forms that took hold in the New World, where they remained popular well into the 1720s.

Huguenot silversmiths, among them Pierre Platel and Pierre Harache, brought a sophisticated sense of proportion and superb craftsmanship to English silver, introducing new forms such as helmet-shaped ewers with cast, embossed, and engraved decoration organized with a controlled sense of formality. While Baroque shapes with cast and chased decoration were characteristic of ecclesiastic and show silver (ewers and basins, cups and covers, and punchbowls and monteiths, or wineglass coolers), simpler decoration, such as gadrooning, that emphasized the elegance of the materials themselves was used in utilitarian household silver (coffeepots, teapots, candlesticks, cups, and tankards).

WOOD

The trunk of the tree is the principal source of wood used by woodworkers in making FURNITURE and useful articles, such as tablewares, toilet articles, and boxes. As the tree develops, the wood nearest the center of the stem, known as "heartwood," ceases to conduct sap and acquires distinctive colors—rich brown in black walnut, deep purple in redcedar, and reddish black in rosewood—which are prized for their beauty. The arrangement of the layers of growth in the tree, as well as the vertical or horizontal orientation of the individual cells, affects the surface appearance (figure) and texture of wood and are loosely described by the word *grain*. The density (weight per unit volume) indicates strength in wood and such characteristics as hardness and ease of nailing and machining. Dense woods generally "move" (shrink or swell) more and are slower to dry. The familiar terms *hardwood* (used for oak, for example) and *softwood* (used for pine and other coniferous trees) do not necessarily indicate their true softness or hardness but relate to their cellular structure or porosity.

Woodworking involves severing, shaping, and surfacing wood with hand or machine tools. Some objects—such as cups, bowls, spoons, and carved sculptures—are made from single pieces of wood; others, such as furniture, are made from more than one piece of wood and joined, held, or glued together or attached by other materials. The junction between two pieces of wood is known as a *joint* and includes worked joints, where the wood is physically interlocked or fitted together (such as mortise and tenon, and dovetail; see FURNITURE); fastened joints, where a fastener such as a dowel or nail is

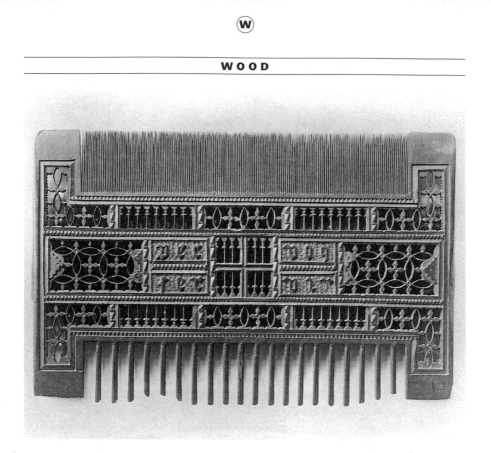

Comb, late 15th or early 16th century. French. Boxwood, length: 7¼ in. (18.3 cm). Philadelphia Museum of Art; Purchased with funds given by Mrs. Edward W. Bok.

attached mechanically to both components; and glued joints, where an adhesive bonds two pieces by surface attachment.

To protect wooden furniture and objects from dirt, abrasion, and moisture and to enhance their appearance, finishes—or transparent coatings—are applied to the surface after it has been prepared. These generally consist of resins dissolved in oil-based solvents; when the solvent evaporates, the resin hardens, adhering firmly to the wood surface. Loosely termed "varnishes," they include shellac, made from natural gum, and lacquer, made from a nitrocellulose resin. Wood can also be treated with oil finishes, such as linseed oil, which soaks into the wood cells, leaving only an imperceptible residue on the exposed surface that enhances the quality of the wood but does not mask it like a varnish.

Wood was used for tablewares in TUDOR times as trenchers or platters for bread and meat, and in the seventeenth century as circular wooden plates of varying sizes. From the seventeenth century, wood was replaced by pewter tablewares in more prosperous households and by ceramics in the eighteenth and nineteenth centuries as native European and American industries developed.

GENERAL

Atterbury, Paul, and Lars Tharp, eds. *The Bulfinch Illustrated Encyclopedia of Antiques.* Boston: Little Brown, Bulfinch, 1994.

Fleming, John, and Hugh Honour. *The Penguin Dictionary of Decorative Arts.* Rev. ed. London: Viking, 1989.

Jervis, Simon. *The Penguin Dictionary of Design and Designers.* Harmondsworth, England: Penguin Books, 1984.

HISTORICAL SURVEYS

Brunhammer, Yvonne, and Suzanne Tise. *French Decorative Art 1900–1942.* Paris: Flammarion, 1990.

Comstock, Helen. *American Furniture: Seventeenth, Eighteenth and Nineteenth Century Styles.* New York: Viking Press, 1962.

Feray, Jean. *Architecture intérieure et décoration en France des origines à 1875.* Paris: Berger-Levrault; Caisse Nationale des Monuments Historiques, 1988.

Gere, Charlotte. *Nineteenth-Century Decoration: The Art of the Interior.* London: Weidenfeld and Nicolson, 1989.

Groer, Leon de. *Decorative Arts in Europe 1790–1850.* New York: Rizzoli, 1986.

Gruber, Alain, ed. *The History of Decorative Arts.* 3 vols. *The Renaissance and Mannerism in Europe* (English translation, 1994) and *Classicism and the Baroque in Europe* (English translation, 1996), New York: Abbeville Press. *Du Néoclassicisme à l'Art Déco* (1994), Paris: Citadelles and Mazenod.

Hansen, Hans Jürgen, ed. *European Folk Art in Europe and the Americas.* London: Thames and Hudson, 1968.

Hiesinger, Kathryn B., and George H. Marcus. *Landmarks of Twentieth-Century Design: An Illustrated Handbook.* New York: Abbeville Press, 1993.

McCorquodale, Charles. *History of the Interior.* New York: Vendome Press, 1983.

Metropolitan Museum of Art, New York. *Nineteenth-Century America: Furniture and Other Decorative Arts.* 1970.

Smith, Charles Saumarez. *Eighteenth-Century Decoration: Design and the Domestic Interior in England.* London: Weidenfeld and Nicolson, 1993.

Thornton, Peter. *Seventeenth-Century Interior Decoration in England, France, and Holland.* New Haven, Conn.: Yale University Press, 1978.

———. *Authentic Decor: The Domestic Interior 1620–1920.* London: Weidenfeld and Nicolson, 1984.

Victoria and Albert Museum, London. *Art and Design in Europe and America 1800–1900.* 1987.

MATERIALS AND TECHNIQUES

Battie, David, ed. *Sotheby's Concise Encyclopedia of Porcelain.* London: Conran Octopus, 1990.

Beard, Geoffrey, and Christopher Gilbert, eds. *Dictionary of English Furniture Makers 1660–1840.* Leeds: Furniture History Society and W. S. Maney and Son, 1986.

Belden, Louise Conway. *Marks of American Silversmiths.* Charlottesville: University Press of Virginia, 1980.

Boyce, Charles. *Dictionary of Furniture.* New York: Henry Holt, 1985.

Britten, F. J. *Old Clocks and Watches and Their Makers.* Woodbridge, England: Antique Collectors' Club, 1977.

Charleston, Robert J., ed. *World Ceramics.* New York: McGraw Hill, 1968.

Cohen, David Harris, and Catherine Hess. *Looking at European Ceramics: A Guide to Technical Terms.* Malibu, Calif.: J. Paul Getty Museum; London: British Museum Press, 1993.

Cooke, Edward S., Jr. *Upholstery in America and Europe from the Seventeenth Century to World War I.* New York: W. W. Norton, 1987.

Cushion, J. P., and W. B. Honey. *Handbook of Pottery and Porcelain Marks.* 3d ed. rev. London: Faber and Faber, 1965.

Danckert, Ludwig. *Directory of European Porcelain: Marks, Makers, and Factories.* London: N.A.G. Press, 1981.

DeVoe, Shirley Spaulding. *English Papier Mâché of the Georgian and Victorian Periods.* Middletown, Conn.: Wesleyan University Press, 1971.

Dictionnaire des horlogers français. 2 vols. Paris: Tardy, 1977–72.

Dillmont, Thérèse de. *The Complete Encyclopedia of Needlework.* 3d ed. Philadelphia: Running Press, 1996.

Edwards, Ralph. *The Dictionary of English Furniture.* Rev. ed. 3 vols. Woodbridge, England: Antique Collectors' Club, 1986.

Fay-Hallé, Antoinette, and Barbara Mundt. *Porcelain of the Nineteenth Century.* New York: Rizzoli, 1983.

Gentle, Rupert, and Rachael Feild. *Domestic Metalwork 1640–1820.* Rev. and enl. Woodbridge, England: Antique Collectors' Club, 1994.

Giusti, Anna Maria. *Pietre Dure: Hardstone in Furniture and Decorations.* London: Philip Wilson, 1992.

Glanville, Philippa. *Silver: History and Design.* New York: Harry N. Abrams, 1996.

Grimwade, Arthur, G. *London Goldsmiths 1697–1837.* 3d rev. and enl. ed. London: Faber and Faber, 1990.

Hapgood, Marilyn Oliver. *Wallpaper and the Artist: From Dürer to Warhol.* New York: Abbeville Press, 1992.

Hayward, Helena, ed. *World Furniture.* New York: McGraw Hill, 1965.

Himmelheber, Georg, and Heinrich Kreisel. *Die Kunst des deutschen Möbels.* 3 vols. Munich: C. H. Beck, 1968–73.

Honour, Hugh. *Cabinet Makers and Furniture Designers.* New York: G. P. Putnam's Sons, 1969.

———. *Goldsmiths and Silversmiths.* London: Weidenfeld and Nicolson, 1971.

Hood, Graham. *American Silver: A History of Style, 1656–1900.*

New York: Praeger Publishers, 1971.

International Hallmarks on Silver. Paris: Tardy, 1985.

Jackson, Radway. *English Pewter Touchmarks.* London: W. Foulsham, 1970.

Kraatz, Anne. *Lace: History and Fashion.* New York: Rizzoli, 1989.

Laughlin, Ledlie I. *Pewter in America: Its Makers and Their Marks.* 2 vols. 1940. Reprint (with a 3d volume of corrections and supplementary information), Barre, Mass.: Barre Publishers, 1969–71.

Ledoux-Lebard, Denise. *Les Ebénistes du XIXe siècle 1795–1889.* Rev. ed. Paris: Les Editions de l'Amateur, 1984.

Lincoln, William A. *World Woods in Color.* Fresno, Calif.: Linden Publishing Co., 1986.

Meister, Peter Wilhelm, and Horst Reber. *European Porcelain of the 18th Century.* Ithaca, N.Y.: Cornell University Press, 1983.

Newman, Harold. *An Illustrated Dictionary of Glass.* London: Thames and Hudson, 1977.

Oman, Charles C., and Jean Hamilton. *Wallpapers: An International History and Illustrated Survey from the Victoria and Albert Museum.* London: Victoria and Albert Museum; New York: Harry N. Abrams, 1982.

Phillips, Barty. *Tapestry.* London: Phaidon Press, 1994.

Pickford, Ian, ed. *Jackson's Silver and Gold Marks of England, Scotland and Ireland.* Woodbridge, England: Antique Collectors' Club, 1989.

Les Poinçons de garantie internationaux pour l'or (et de platine). Paris: Tardy, 1969.

Les Poinçons des étains français. Paris: Tardy, 1968.

Pradère, Alexandre. *French Furniture Makers: The Art of the Ebéniste from Louis XIV to the Revolution.* Malibu, Calif.: J. Paul Getty Museum, 1989.

Sherrill, Sarah B. *Carpets and Rugs of Europe and America.* New York: Abbeville Press, 1996.

Tait, Hugh, ed. *Five Thousand Years of Glass.* London: British Museum Press, 1991.

Truman, Charles, ed. *Sotheby's Concise Encyclopedia of Silver.* London: Conran Octopus, 1996.

Wechssler-Kümmel, S. *Chandeliers, lampes et appliques de style.* Fribourg: Office du Livre, 1963.

CONSERVATION

Jackson, Albert, and David Day. *Care and Repair of Furniture*. London: Harper Collins Publishers, 1994.

James, David. *Upholstery: A Complete Course*. Lewes, England: Guild of Master Craftsman Publications, 1990.

Schultz, Arthur W., ed. *Caring for Your Collections*. New York: Harry N. Abrams, 1992.

Simpson, Mette Tang, and Michael Huntley, eds. *Sotheby's Caring for Antiques: A Guide to Handling, Cleaning, Display, and Restoration*. London: Conran Octopus, 1996.

COLLECTING

Christie's Review of the Season. London: Christie's. Published annually.

Miller's International Antiques Price Guide: Professional Handbook. London: Miller's. Published annually.

Sotheby's Art at Auction: The Year in Review. London: Conran Octopus. Published annually.

Page numbers in *italics* refer to illustrations.
Page numbers in **boldface** refer to the main entry for that term.

PHOTOGRAPHY CREDITS

The photographers and the sources of the photographic material other than those indicated in the captions are as follows:

Copyright © Art Resource, New York, pages 108, 111;
copyright © Harold Corsini/The Collection of the Frick Art Museum, Pittsburgh, Pennsylvania, page 193;
copyright © John Hammond/National Trust Photographic Library, Derbyshire, England, page 32;
copyright © Hubert Josse/Abbeville Press, New York, pages 12, 14, 18, 23, 79;
copyright © Lynn Rosenthal/Philadelphia Museum of Art, page 99;
copyright © Graydon Wood/Philadelphia Museum of Art, pages 75, 119, 153, 164.

Front cover, left: *Armchair*, c. 1750–60. See page 64.

Front cover, center: Albert Cheuret (n.d.). *Clock*, c. 1930. See page 24.

Front cover, right: Dominik Biemann (1800–1857). *Lidded Tumbler*, 1830–31. See page 47.

Back cover: *Flask or Flagon*, c. 1545–50. See page 9.

Half-title: Benjamin Pyne (active 1676–1732) and Peter Archambo
(active 1721–67). *Kettle, Cream Pitcher, and Sugar Box*, 1720–22.
See page 146.

Frontispiece: Van der Voorst (n.d.) after François Boucher (1703–1770).
The Jealous Suitor, c. 1756. See page 175.

Editor: Nancy Grubb
Designer: Scott W. Santoro/WORKSIGHT
Typesetting/Layout: Emily L. Santoro/WORKSIGHT
Production Editor: Owen Dugan
Picture Editor: Laura Straus
Production Manager: Lou Bilka

First edition
10 9 8 7 6 5 4 3 2 1

Library of Congress Cataloging-in-Publication Data
Hiesinger, Kathryn B., 1943–
    Antiquespeak : a guide to the styles, techniques, and materials of the decorative arts, from
    the Renaissance to art deco / Kathryn B. Hiesinger and George H. Marcus.
        p. cm.
    Includes index.
    ISBN 0-7892-0189-5. — ISBN 0-7892-0337-5 (pbk.)
    1. Decorative arts—Dictionaries. 2. Antiques—Dictionaries.
    I. Marcus, George H. II. Title.
NK30.H56 1997
745.1'03—dc21   97-10513